On the Way to Feed the Swans

a Memoir by
Hannelore Hahn

Tenth House Enterprises, Inc., New York

Grateful acknowledgement is made to:
Helen Hahn, for most family photographs
M. Hofmann, for supplying views of Dresden
Jakob Levy, Bernard Maier, Bruno Stern, for photos and information on *Veda*.

For permission to reprint illustrations:
Dance Collection: The New York Public Library at Lincoln Center
LIFE Picture Collection
The Museum of Modern Art—Collection and Film Stills Archives
George A. Tice

Grateful acknowledgement is made to friends, old and new:
Lynn Bales, Margarete Bernhardt, Evelyn DeMarco, Tessa Devonald, Veronica Foley,
Ati Forberg, Joel S. Forman, Doris C. Freedman, Ainslie Dinwiddie Grannis,
Letty Grierson, Dorothy Hansen, Victoria J. Richardson Heland, Walter Heller,
Greta Hofmann-Nemiroff, Ruth Atwood Janas, Eleanor Johnson, Felix Klein,
Leo Lerman, Ruth Limmer, Nancy McManus, Jonas Mekas, D.H. Melhem,
Virginia Parsell, Kay Sinclair, L.C. Stoumen, Nancy Strode, John Wallen.

Copyright © Hannelore Hahn, 1982
All rights reserved
First published in 1982 by Tenth House Enterprises, Inc.,
Box 810, Gracie Station, New York, NY 10028

Library of Congress Card Number: 82-99824
ISBN: 0-9603310-3-4
Printed in the United States of America

Set in: Aldine Roman
Graphics: D. Bruce Zahor Design
Typographer: Aenjai Graphic Studio
Printer: Colombia Graphic Arts
Editors: Letty Grierson, Tatiana Stoumen
Calligrapher: William Metzig
Front cover photo credit: Hugo Jaeger, LIFE Magazine, ○ Time Inc.

*. . . and special thanks
for love and support to:*

*Ellen Resch
and
John R. Lawrence*

*To my mother and
my daughter, Tatiana*

Author's Note

I am inclined to liken the writing of this book to the shaping of a bell. Everyone has his bell. This is to say, we all have our individual lives and those things which have happened to us. And even though we shape this material into a bell and put a clapper to it, it might not ring at all, or at best make only a dull sound.

Facts alone do not make a story. Plot is a device for the writers of fiction. But an autobiography which plots the course of one's life must have a ring to it—a timbre, a cadence.

At the beginning, that special sound may just be heard inside your head and only for a moment. Something may occur to you, as in a dream, except you sense it was not a dream, but a visitation. Such moments are rare and fleeting. Generally, the geology of our lives is a layered mass—a labyrinthed mineshaft of compressed memory, charred meteors imbedded in brain cells. Still, in order to write recollectively, these blackened nodules must be visited. Then, when contact is made, they must be sensed beyond personal property and reset within a landscape whose topography may be traveled by all.

What has helped me was the image of the earth as seen from outer space by the astronauts. A new view of something very familiar, a distant perch. This gave perspective to the canvas.

What also helped was the continual buffing of the bell. The continual working of the material from the inside. It was the sound I heard from a section which had been buffed right, that kept me going.

It took a long time to ring the bell.

Hannelore Hahn
New York City
May 1982

By New York time it was seven in the morning. I had been traveling for thirteen hours and had eaten twice on the plane. But who could refuse lunch in an elegant Swiss dining car on its way from Zurich to Milan?

The Italian-speaking head waiter seated me next to two Swiss ladies and inquired if I would have some wine.

Salute!

The dining car ritual which has been described and redescribed in countless books and depicted in movies, had begun. Between sips of Beaujolais, I watched the scenery at my window change like the courses on the menu. Swiss chalets dotted with red geraniums were followed by Oxtail *Claire en Tasse*. Green meadows surrounded by snow-capped mountains came with *Cote de Veau Milanaise*, gulps of blue lakes and *Spritzers* of white waterfalls. And, between bites, there were tunnels to give the eyes and stomach a moment of rest.

In an hour and a half I would be in Lugano where, at the Kurhaus C., I had arranged to meet Hertha. When I was a child she had served in our household in Dresden as a cook and nanny and had, despite Nazism, Fascism and Communism, not to mention the fire bombing and destruction of Dresden itself, maintained a loving contact with my family, particularly with me whom she had loved as her child. This connection was never severed.

"Do you remember," she would write, "When you and I had breakfast on Sundays by ourselves on the kitchen balcony? Your *Pappi* and *Mutti* still slept, of course, but we had the world to ourselves." Or,

> Do you remember the day I sent you to the greengrocer to get some parsley and you came back with a bagful of old lettuce? I was just about to scold you, but then I found the parsley at the very bottom of the bag. Herr Benke told me

later that you had asked him to put the old lettuce on top to play a trick on me. 'Fill the bag up with some rotten vegetables,' you had said to him, 'so Hertha will think I brought the wrong thing.' Oh, you were a devil. But those were good times, the best times of my life. If only Hitler hadn't come, I would still be with you.

The train stopped in Lugano. Soon we would meet. Our first meeting in forty years.

At the Kurhaus C., the young women behind the desk requested to see my American passport. Had Frl. Baumann already arrived, I inquired between these formalities.

"No," the registration clerk said. "She will not be coming."

"Not be coming?" I repeated in disbelief. "You mean not at all?"

"The Kurhaus received a card from Frl. Baumann only yesterday," the woman explained, "canceling her arrival." Sensing my distress, she went to get the card. It was dated August 23, 1979 and was written in German.

> I must regretfully cancel my reservation at your hotel. Our East German authorities require, besides name of hotel, city and country, the exact street address, and since this was not indicated in your brochure, nor on your letterhead, permission for me to leave Dresden was not granted by the police.
>
> P.S. Unfortunately, it is now too late to rectify this situation, for even if you were to supply the street name and number, it would be to no avail, since the process for obtaining permission to travel takes six weeks. I am very sad.
> H. Baumann

At dawn on Sunday mornings, I used to crawl into Hertha's bed with my story book. She would read to me until we decided to have breakfast. Then she would fix herself a cup of *Blümchen Kaffee*, or "little flower coffee." Dresden, which was rightfully famous for many things, was renowned for its coffee. Its renown however had nothing to do with the coffee's potency or taste. The name originated from the cups in which the coffee was served. They had little flowers painted at the bottom. In other words, the Dresden coffee was so weak one could always see the little flower through it.

All Saxon habits were geared to slow down the metabolism. Like the fable of "The Hare and the Tortoise," the people of Dresden and those who lived in its province, called Saxony, were the tortoises of Germany.

Besides their coffee, Saxons were particularly made fun of because of the way they talked. Their dialect sent people from other parts of the country into howls of laughter. Saxon-German was German spoken at the slowest possible speed.

But if the people of Saxony were slow, they were also patient and spent time taking care of things. Someone was always in the process of buffing shoes, doorknobs and the rich veneered wood of Biedermeier furniture. I suppose that is why, when I took my first steps, I did not walk toward my mother, or my father, or my nurse, but I waddled toward the shiny black boots of our chauffeur, Herr Stitterich. He really knew how to put a sheen on them.

Growing up in Saxony gave you the feeling that nothing bad would ever happen, if only because everyone moved too slowly to cause a sudden accident.

Karl Stitterich was in every sense of the word a Saxon. As a chauffeur he hugged the road, tortoise-style; his interpretation of motion being not the gas pedal, but the brakes.

The car we had at the time was a lightweight, four-door sedan called *Wanderer*. It had delicate, even streamlined contours. No matter; Stitterich drove this sleek auto as if it were a trailer truck stacked with highly inflammable cargo. This caution, however, also made him a very responsible driver and earned him the Knight of the Road medal for aiding motorists while on overnight business trips with my father. A black iron cross, signifying acts of heroism on the *Autobahn*, was proudly attached to the rear bumper of our car.

My father kept proof of his own heroism in a tan pigskin *étui*. These were the medals he had earned in the First World War, while fighting for Germany against the French. He had been a prisoner of war and had escaped, disguised as a woman, by jumping off a moving train. I always thought it strange when I heard it mentioned that my father as a young man looked very much like a girl. It was said that he had no beard and that he fainted at the sight of blood.

By the time I had any judgment on the matter, which was, maybe, at the age of four, I thought he was the handsomest of men. True, he wasn't tall, but he was tall to me, a mere smidgen of a child, and he had pale blue eyes which changed to gray depending on the color of the silk necktie he was wearing. My father was vain and probably owned more custom-tailored suits, shirts, ties and shoes than any man I have known since. He also had his nails manicured regularly, taking pride in the fact that the white "moon" was visible on each finger. Good-looking hands, he always said, were a trait that came from his side of the family. So did strong genes. Any weaknesses, particularly mental maladies, were attributed by him to my mother's side, the non-Germans. The Austrians. The Brachs.

But most of all, my father was extremely sensual. Good food was of utmost importance. His favorite sensations came from things which could be sucked and would slide down your throat without chewing. Like white asparagus imported in cans from Belgium, for example. Or very tender pink veal.

In the same category of importance were, of course, women. One of my earliest childhood memories involves his taking me on a visit to the apartment of an attractive dark-haired woman named Rita. Her hair was pulled back Spanish-style and she wore bold jewelry and hoop earrings. She was very different looking from any of the women in my family and even had an emerald green parrot. Just who this woman was in my father's life, I was not told of course. But I grew up with the notion that my father had "loves" and that my mother wasn't really one of them. But I, at the age of four or five, was.

Hertha, too, had a crush on him. She could not bear having to leave us when Hitler proclaimed that servants in Jewish households had to be thirty-six years old, or older. Hertha was only thirty-two.

Oh, yes, we were Jewish.

The only one in my family who was conscious of being Jewish was my father. Perhaps if his father had not been orthodox and there had not been anti-semitism in his hometown, my father would have been oblivious too. But the people of that small Hessian town called Hersfeld, where until 1866 no Jews were allowed to live (even those who worked there during the day had to live in the surrounding villages), would not let him forget what he was. He was a "Jew boy," no matter how hard he tried to fight for his country in World War I; no matter how many decorations he earned for his acts of heroism. No matter. The small towns of Germany harbored anti-semitism long before Hitler. Weren't the Jews accused of contaminating the village fountains with disease and pox in medieval days? Well, these were medieval towns. It was an endemic, inbred prejudice against which there was no antibiotic.

But Dresden, where I was born, was not a medieval town. As a seat of art and culture, it was more related to the Renaissance than to any other period in history. The residents of late eighteenth and nineteenth-century Dresden included such names of German romanticism as the painter Casper David Friedrich, the

Clockwise from above:
Dresden on the Elbe
Hannelore and her father at a swimming p
  in Dresden
Dix, Otto
  Dr. Mayer-Hermann. 1926
  Oil and tempra on wood. Collection,
  Museum of Modern Art, New York
  Gift of Philip Johnson
Terrine decorated with onion pattern.
  Porcelain collection, Dresden-Zwinger
Wallpavillion, Dresden-Zwinger
The *Palais* in the *Grosse Garten*, Dresden
Hannelore at age 4 in Dresden

Mary Wigman, courtesy of the Dance Collection, The New York Public Library at Lincoln Center

Hannelore at age 6.
  "That year I auditioned for the *Corps de Ballet* at the Dresden State Opera House." Photo credit: Genja Jonas

poet Friedrich Schiller, and the composers Carl Maria von Weber, Robert Schumann, and Richard Wagner. And as an ethnographic region, Saxony was more closely related to the Slavic peoples, who were its early settlers, than to any Germanic tribes. This natural relationship to Eastern Europe gave this region a very different cast than other parts of Germany, such a Bavaria, or Prussia, for example, with which Germany is more commonly identified.

This great city of three-quarters of a million people also had a unique tolerance for both the old and the new. In the 1920s modern dance, for example, was cradled in Dresden. Mary Wigman, Palucca, and Hanya Holm exerted an international influence on dance everywhere, including on Martha Graham in the United States.

I started to dance at the age of four and went to a castle in the old part of town to take my lessons. Herr Dietz, my ballet teacher, had a studio there. It was a bare room, except for a *barre* and two tall windows which let in a gray north light. The castle had no heat or electricity, and when my fellow students and I took our lessons there in the late afternoons, the chill empty space filled with the deep tones of a Rembrandt painting.

One day, when I was doing the split, I accidentally peed, puppylike, on the castle floor. I was five years old. A year later, I auditioned for the *Corps de Ballet* at the Dresden State Opera House. Most likely, I was the youngest candidate ever to audition there. My mother had just filled out the application form. The *Corps de Ballet* maestro glanced it over, then apologetically handed it back to her. The Company, being state-supported, could not accept Jews. A year earlier, this would not have been a problem. It had never been a question before.

I suppose, had this not been the case, I would have become a dancer. When you start that early, how can you miss?

When I first saw Hitler, he was standing on the roof of a car making a speech. My mother and I had been on our way to feed the swans in the *Grosse Garten*, Dresden's magnificent park, when suddenly the real Hitler appeared before us. He had apparently come into town to visit an important *Gauleiter*, a precinct leader, in front of whose house he addressed an impromptu crowd. His visit had not been announced, but passersby were attracted by a black and silver Mercedes. Two red, white and black swastika flags flew from delicate silver stanchions which were attrached to each fender. They wondered *"was für ein grosses Tier"* had come to town? Few if any probably guessed it was Adolf himself.

Maharanis wearing golden saris and red dots on their foreheads often came. I had seen such exotic visitors in the lobby of Dresden's Hotel Westminster. And flocks of graceful birds sometimes stopped in Dresden, too, on their way to points south. Widows and landladies in Dresden were especially partial to parrots. They taught them to speak in the Saxon dialect.

I had a canary. I called him Hänschen or "little Hans." Most canaries were called that. Dresden was not a city for dogs.

Well, there was Hitler standing on top of a black and silver car, like the devil just popped out of hell. My mother immediately pulled me away as if I were about to witness a lewd act in a circus sideshow—the nude lady fornicating with a gorilla, for example. I knew I was not to look back or I would be turned into stone or maybe a pillar of salt. And I didn't. But that scene stayed with me always. It was like seeing something you knew you were not supposed to watch. A magic act. A fakir playing with snakes. What is more impressive than watching danger?

Now you see it. Now you don't.

And where does one see such things?

In far away places. Or when the circus comes to town. Or on the outskirts, where the gypsies set up tent.

Here today. Gone tomorrow.

Never at home.

I will return to this period in time. But first, I want to relate a few things about the time before. For it was my parents' time and their parents' time, which really set the stage.

My father was born in 1899. He was barely seventeen years old when he became a *Frontsoldat*, a soldier at the Front, fighting against the French in the First World War. Although he might have been drafted at this early age, since Germany had had severe losses, the story is that my father volunteered to fight for his country with the enthusiasm and idealism for which those who knew him in those days still remembered him sixty years later.

Even though he had been awarded the Iron Cross, all I ever heard him say of this period in his life was that he had been taken prisoner by the French and that he had escaped from a moving train dressed as a woman. He never mentioned any of the men with whom he had shared these experiences, nor gave any further details of what happened to him during those years of his life. By the time I came into the world, that chapter was closed. But the missing pieces of the escape anecdote added up to something like this:

My father, according to some of his friends, had actually escaped twice. The first time he was recaptured and sent to a prisoner-of-war camp, where, for the amusement of the French officers, the German prisoners were asked to put on theatrical performances—Moliere in the trenches, so to speak. My father, who was one of the youngest prisoners and beardless, was given the female roles. This in itself would not have been so bad, but in the circumstance of war, offstage advances were made to him by the men, both French and German—a disclosure he made years later to my mother, with deep personal revulsion.

While on stage, as the innocent *femme* however, he attracted the attention of the mistress of a French colonel, who was herself an actress in the *Comedie Francaise*. She brought him to the particular attention of the mature-in-years French colonel, who made him his orderly. Although the war ended in 1918, my father continued to serve as the colonel's orderly, since reparations between the Germans and the French were very slow and the exchange of prisoners-of-war became a long, drawn-out affair. Besides, my father had become the lover of the colonel's young mistress. She called him most affectionately "le petit Artur," and he wore her clothing when he jumped off the moving train.

C'est la guerre.

When my father finally returned from the war in 1919, Kaiser Wilhelm had already fled to Holland and the German/Prussian monarchy, which had risen under Bismarck since the 1860s, was no more. The Weimar Republic, Germany's attempt at a more representative and constitutional government, was trying out its fragile wings, while birds of prey, Communism and Fascism, waited in the political wings to destroy Germany's attempt at a democratic government at the first possible opportunity.

It was during this brief break between two extremes, the German monarchy on the one hand and National Socialism under Hitler on the other (a period of less than twenty years), that my father went to the University of Würzburg to study law.

How quickly history is forgotten! By the time I was born it seemed that going to the university was a most natural thing to do. Yet less than 100 years earlier, Jews did not attend German universities nor had they risen into the middle and upper middle classes. Ironically, the German-Jewish economic and professional rise into German society went hand in hand with the rise of the German Empire, and the rise of the German Empire in the mid-nineteenth century was a natural result of what was happening the world over: the rise of industry and capitalism and its clash with the hitherto agrarian status quo. In the United States in the 1860s, for example, the clash was most poignantly brought home in the War between the States, when the industrial North and agrarian South could no longer co-exist. At the same time, in Germany, the industrial revolution brought about the rise of the German Empire under Bismarck.

Prior to 1860, Germany had consisted of more than two dozen independent states, each ruled by an aristocratic landed gentry in a semi-feudalistic fashion. Although attempts toward the unification of these separate states had been made at various times in history, such a unification did not really come about until Otto von Bismarck took office as Kaiser Wilhelm's chancellor. Bismarck was himself of the aristocratic landed gentry, and he envisioned a strongly united Germany under Prussia as an essential step toward the new economic and political power. Until then, France and Austria were the two ruling powers on the Continent and Germany had yet to make its mark. In the eyes of Bismarck, unification had to be based on military might. "Blood and Iron" was his slogan. Time and again however the more agrarian members of the German Parliament refused to approve his accelerated military budgets. Not being a natural parliamentarian himself, Bismarck sought other means for obtaining funds. This search led him to a German-Jewish banker named Bleichröder, who was later knighted for enabling Bismarck to accomplish his dream. Gerson von Bleichröder floated the necessary loans to finance three militaristically and politically crucial wars: first against Denmark, then against France, and lastly against Austria. All the while he was building a close relationship with the Paris and London Rothschilds, who had been clearly the center for moneylending to the monarchs of Europe for the past 100 years.

And so it was that the unification and rise of the German Empire came about through a close partnership between Bismarck and Bleichröder, a Prussian Junker and a German Jew.

Yet, of the approximately seven thousand works which had appeared about Bismarck, hardly any even mention Bleichröder. In 1977 a Columbia University history professor named Fritz Stern published his book, *Gold and Iron: Bismarck and Bleichröder, the Building of the German Empire*, revealing the story as never told before.

During the time of the unique Bismarck/Bleichröder partnership, new economic opportunities opened for all of Germany. With them came the legal emancipation of the German Jews, which meant they could own property and enter the professions and, as was the case in my father's hometown, the new Prussian state allowed Jews to actually live in Bad Hersfeld, not just work there. The doors of the German universities were also opened to them and it became the fervent desire of every Jewish family to send at least one son to study. No wonder that some sixty-five years later all the Jews my family knew were either doctors, lawyers, or businessmen with university degrees.

When I came upon the scene in the late 1920s, everyone acted as though this had always been the case. Yet, the parents of those educated Jews never went to the university. And the parents before them? No one talked about that. They truly lived in a different time, a time when the Jews in Germany were a small, vulnerable minority of moneylenders and middlemen in continuous need of protection from the lords and barons of the separate agrarian states who were not allowed legally or professionally to be integrated into German society.

For my father, going to the university was certainly the obvious next step toward professional advancement and social integration. He had served his country well during the war and his deeds did not go unrecognized. His country had awarded him the Iron Cross and other medals and he firmly believed that these would henceforth protect him from any anti-semitism and discrimination. The innate feeling of vulnerability based on his Jewishness was momentarily assuaged; so much so, that he became a fervent speaker for the German-Jewish war veterans organization, the *Deutsch-Jüdische Frontsoldaten*. In ardent speeches at regional meetings, he told his German-Jewish brothers not to convert to

Christianity but to remain proud Jews, for they had nothing to fear anymore.

They had had a chance to fight for their country and to demonstrate their loyalty and love for it. This demonstration, he insisted, Germany would never forget. Thus, he implored, they were safe, as their fathers and their father's fathers had never been.

Actually, at the time of the First World War, there were five hundred and fifty thousand Jews living in what was then considered the German national territory. Of these five hundred and fifty thousand, one hundred thousand served in the war and of these, eighty thousand fought in the front lines. Of these eighty thousand who fought at the Front, twelve thousand German Jews lost their lives.

Germany on the other hand did not wish to make too much of the enormous Jewish support it received in the war and, contrary to its usual punctiliousness about facts and figures, did not keep a precise count. The record keeping was left for Jewish organizations to do, who had them subsequently approved officially.

After returning from the war in 1919, my father entered the University of Würzburg with hope and eagerness. He truly believed a new and very propitious time lay ahead and he chose jurisprudence as the means of securing his future. I suppose he selected law because it was the most practical of the various studies offered. He was not at all inclined toward the sciences. His nature was sentimental, emotional, yet shrewd. His mind tended toward immediate application and his emotions toward quick gratification. He was capable of swaying others more through sheer emotional appeal than by the drier and less personal steps of logic and demonstrative proof. Most important, my father was impatient, impatient to become socially prominent and powerful above all else. And this *Sturm und Drang* had to be combined by him, sooner or later, with a way of acquiring wealth.

Life in the German universities at the time was one part studies and two parts participation in the colorful and rigorous life of the student fraternities. Of the four fraternities at the University of Würzburg; Veda, Salia, Rheno-Palatia and Wirceburgia, whose membership was mixed with Jews, non-Jews and converted Jews, he chose the all-Jewish Veda. (As sailors refer to their ships as "she," so the German university students likewise endowed their fraternities with the feminine gender and gave them the German article *die*.)

Die Veda was the Sanskrit word for knowledge. Her colors—white, green and red—were worn in grosgrain as a watch fob and at major social functions as a broad sash across the chest.

Fraternity dress uniforms were meticulous copies of the nineteenth century uniforms of the Hussars, the military officers of the Austro-Hungarian Empire—later seen on the stage of twentieth century operettas.

At afternoon teas and annual balls, the eligible sisters, female relatives and friends of the young men were invited and introduced around in the fraternity houses. Obviously, a young woman paid enormous attention to the dates of the fraternity functions, for these were her best and possibly only chances to find a husband who could promise her an upper-middle-class life. My father's sister, Berti, for example, along with her mother, my grandmother Julia, spent many hours at the dressmaker having elaborate outfits made for each of these occasions. The story goes that *Opa* Jakob, the banker, had to float a loan in order to pay for all this finery.

Die Veda, like the other fraternities, had her own house where the students spent long hours talking, singing and drinking in *der Kneipe*, the pub. All fraternity brothers had to drink, although drunkenness was strictly forbidden. The code of that time and place required of the young men who were "in training," so to speak, to hold future positions of leadership that they should show they could hold their liquor, not by moderation but by total and rigorous participation in drinking rituals. No other liquor but beer was served, and it was consumed in night-long socials interspersed with boisterous bursts of song.

It was a sign of weakness not be be able to hold one's liquor.

Upper left:
Bad Hersfeld, Hessia, where my father was born
My father as a young man, circa 1916
Lower left:
"... that new life, engendered by the rapid rise of early twentieth-
century industry was 'in the air'..."
The Cabinet of Dr Caligari," The Museum of Modern Art/Film Stills Archive
Above:
Members of the *Veda*. Fraternity, University of Würzburg, circa 1920/21.
My father is standing in second row, extreme right.
Right:
Oma Julia in later years

Thus, when the young men seemed dangerously close to reaching a stage of intoxication, they would go into one of the fraternity's special bathrooms equipped with hot and cold showers. After showering, they re-emerged and joined their brothers for more rounds of song and beer, just as long as they did not pass out. That would indeed be a shameful indication that they "did not have what it takes."

But the most intensive tests for showing "mettle" were the duels. Dueling with swords and sabers was a most important tradition of German university life. Although outlawed by the Weimar Republic, at the time my father entered the university it was nevertheless carried on in secret in an old brewery, where a thick layer of sawdust was used to obscure all evidence of human blood. For this same reason, the participants wore patent leather shoes which allowed for a thorough wiping off. For their safety, they donned leather aprons and wore masks for the protection of neck and eyes.

Dueling took place for two reasons: first as an initiation rite to show the courage of those pledgees (or "foxes" as they were called) who wished to join the fraternity; and second to restore honor threatened by a slight or insult.

Both kinds of duels were staged strictly behind closed doors and carried out according to precise rules and regulations. Two kinds of weapons were used: *der Schläger*, a straight sword, and *das Schwert*, a small saber whose blade (ten inches from the tip) was razor sharp. The blades of the swords and sabers had to be kept completely sterile and so could not strike the floor. A doctor was always present. So was a "second" or adjutant for each man, who saw to it that the dueling rounds were brief, or no more than twelve to fifteen strokes, and that things were generally kept in check. Deaths did however occur.

Since only university men were allowed to duel and prove their Teutonic knightly prowess, a dueling scar on the cheek, like the cut of a jib, was a mark of social standing or "class."

My father would never have met my mother if his mother, my grandmother, *Oma* Julia, had not one day plucked a goose.

As family legend would have it, *Oma* Julia was sitting in her kitchen in the little Hessian town of Bad Hersfeld, plucking the feathers out of a goose, when her eyes fell upon an ad in the newspaper which she had spread under the goose's rump. The ad invited any German-Jewish male of good background and with legal training to send his references to a box number. Object: matrimony and family business partnership.

The ad had been placed by my mother's father, my grandfather, *Opa* Brach. *Opa* and *Oma* Brach and their three children were German-speaking Austrians living in Czechoslovakia, which previous to World War I belonged to the Austro-Hungarian Empire. There in the Moravian town of Olomouc , *Opa* Brach owned the *Hanna Maltzfabrik* which he had inherited from his father, my great grandfather, who had started out as a dealer in grain.

At the end of the first World War, *Opa* Brach expanded his business by buying a second malthouse. This one was situated on the River Elbe, near the city of Dresden in the eastern part of Germany. Leaving his younger brother in charge of the *Hanna Maltzfabrik* in Czechoslovakia in the early 1920s, *Opa* Brach and my grandmother *Oma* Louise moved with their children, Erna, Fredie and my mother Helene, to Dresden and settled into an imposing town house always respectfully referred to thereafter as "Bergstrasse Number 16."

Since all executive positions in the family malt business were held by relatives and *Opa* Brach's brother, *Onkel* Robert, had remained in Olomouc , my grandfather now cast about for someone suitable to marry into the family and to manage the new German branch.

Family ties on my mother's side were so close that her immediate family in Olomouc actually lived together in what was called *das Familien Haus* (the family house), which was in fact a kind of family condominium where relatives owned spacious apartments on different floors.

My grandfather's sisters, *Tante* Malwiene and *Tante* Ida, occupied the first and third floors respectively. *Tante* Malwiene's husband was an engineer and *Tante* Ida's husband was a doctor. *Onkel* Robert, my grandfather's younger brother, lived with his wife, *Tante* Steffi, on the second floor. As my grandfather's business partner, he had the most luxurious of the three apartments in the *Familien Haus.* He was an art collector and owned a famous Breughel, a painting of villagers skating on a pond. Their older son, Eric, served in the Czech Army and later entered the malt business. His younger brother, Herbert, was sent to study at the Massachusetts Institute of Technology in "Amerika." In the early 1930s, he was probably the only young man from Olomouc who went there. Herbert later became an executive of an American petroleum company in Mexico City.

At the time I visited the "family condo" in Olomouc , I was too young to realize how unusual this set-up was. Not too young however to make the rounds from floor to floor to eat. The *Familien Haus* was like a dry-docked luxury liner whose only purpose seemed to be to turn out heavenly baked goods and desserts. *Tante* Malwiene's *Apfelstrudl* was served hot with whipped cream, in the middle of the afternoon *zum Kaffee; Tante* Ida's *Kipferln*, small horn-shaped butter cookies, were strewn with powered sugar; *Tante* Steffi's *Linzertorte,* was an almond cake layered with strawberry marmalade, and so on forever.

The *Hanna Maltzfabrik*, squatting in a field of wheat and poppies, boasted a fertile orchard and vegetable garden. The best cherries came from there. So did asparagus which was grown under glass. My aunts placed their orders for fresh fruits and vegetables with Novak, the malthouse gardener, fructifying my childhood impression that factories were benign family enterprises located in the country, whose grounds produced delicious edibles which city children, like me, could pluck and take home to aunts and maids who would preserve them in jars as compotes, jellies and marmalades, or bake them into cakes.

Novak was also the chauffeur for *Onkel* Robert and *Tante* Steffi. He drove their tan Buick with the top down and wore a white duster and goggles. The goggles were to keep the dust out of his eyes, since the Czech roads were notoriously less well paved than their German counterparts. Novak was fond of speeding and talked engagingly while driving. His broad smile prominently revealed a gold front tooth, a mark of the east European dentistry at the time. Stitterich had no gold teeth, but then he did not flash broad smiles either. With him one had to sit in utter silence. He could not talk and drive at the same time.

The house my father grew up in with his two brothers; Isfried, the eldest, Rudi, the youngest, and his beauteous sister Berti also had three floors. The family lived in the middle, on the second floor. Downstairs was the family's business, which was a small private bank. It consisted of one large room, steel safes, and many wooden drawers with grooves into which variously sized coins fitted snugly. One of the grooves was reserved for gold coins.

The third floor of my father's house was rented out. In the back of the house, thirty chickens laid eggs.

In the morning, my grandfather, *Opa* Jakob, did not have far to go to the two places which concerned him the most: his bank and his synagogue. One was downstairs, the other, the *Schul*, was across the street. Downstairs and across the street was just about as far as he wished to go. He did not concern himself with anything beyond. Before breakfast, *Opa* Jakob would walk across the street to the synagogue for morning prayers. He and the few other Jewish men of this small Hessian community would don black skullcaps and white shawls edged in black. They said prayers in Hebrew and sometimes broke out in wails. Women were left with the work in the house and did not go to morning prayer. But, if they had gone, they would have had to sit in the upstairs gallery, as they did on high holidays. The house of worship was strictly segregated.

At the conclusion of morning prayers, *Opa* Jakob would walk back across the street into his house for breakfast. There he would dunk fresh poppyseed rolls into his coffee cup and, leaving heaps of crusty crumbs on the breakfast table, he would go downstairs and pull the heavy iron shutters from the windows of his bank. The Jakob Hahn *Bankgeschäft* was now open for business.

Downstairs and across the street was not enough for my grandmother, *Oma* Julia. She deeply wished she could go beyond the precise circumference of her home, but the farthest she could venture was to the edge of town where she kept a vegetable garden. There she went every day with a pot full of chicken manure with which she fertilized the ground. The tiny plot of land was so fully packed that it was difficult to find a place to set one's feet. Hardy German vegetables, such as red and green cabbage, potatoes, tomatoes, cucumbers, radishes, beets, yellow and green beans grew there in happy profusion, as did delicate sweet peas and fruit trees whose seasonal bounty was so generous that their heavy branches had to be propped up. The garden was precisely rimmed by a fence—heavily overgrown by hedge roses which made the weather-beaten wooden garden door hard to find. The door opened with a large key which my grandmother carried in her apron pocket. In a small shed bordered by smiling sunflowers, rusted garden tools rested amid spider webs.

There in the quiet of mid-afternoon, my grandmother would sow seeds, pull weeds, sprinkle water from a large can, loosen top soil and harvest green peas, red cherries, purple plums, or whatever was ready to be plucked from this loyal horn of plenty.

In that special quiet, with only butterflies, caterpillars, earthworms and snails as her mute companions, she would think about her children and where they might live one day if they could find their way out of what seemed to her—and to them as they grew older—a hemmed-in existence. If they could make their way into the big cities, such as Berlin, Frankfurt, Munich, or Dresden, she at least would be able to visit them and partake of that new and more interesting life.

Although that new life, engendered by the rapid rise of

early 20th century industry, hadn't yet transformed the small towns and villages, it was "in the air" and tickled the nostrils of small-town people, as salt does horses.

Orphaned in early life, *Oma* Julia married my grandfather, as had been arranged by her relatives. Although she dutifully performed her wifely tasks, her life lay heavy upon her ample chest. She often heaved sighs and tears rolled down her rosy checks for no reason. She seemingly had everything that was her due, or considered the due of a woman of her place and time. Yet it can be said she was not happy. The world was changing. Things were going on she wanted to be a part of. And something oppressed her: the harshness with which her husband ruled the home. Too much obedience. She could not bear it when he struck the boys.

When in 1925, *Oma* Julia chanced upon the ad calling for a "young Jewish male with legal training" in the newspaper lying under the rump of the goose she was preparing for dinner, she knew she had a candidate. Neither her eldest son, Isfried, nor her youngest son, Rudi, had gone to the university. But her middle son, Arthur, had the right "cut" this opportunity called for.

Just how my father made contact with my mother's family remains shrouded in conjecture, particularly since another version of how he met my mother obfuscates the story of the newspaper ad. This second version however in no way changes my father's basic motivation: to get rich and powerful as quickly as possible.

Instead of the ad, which relatives on my mother's side disclaim but which relatives on my father's side insist on, the story goes like this: After graduation from the University of Würzburg in 1923, Arthur Hahn clearly wished to make his way in business rather than law. The degree he had received was an academic law degree, but in order to become a full-fledged lawyer, he had to spend several more years of work in the courts and for other lawyers, as well as take additional examinations. This was clearly not for him. He decided instead to work as an accountant for a firm in the town of Kassel, but soon took an interim job in his father's bank. Things were just not happening fast enough for him. He felt exceedingly restless and, in the summer of 1925, he decided to take a vacation trip outside his native country, to Czechoslovakia.

Thus it happened that, sitting at the bar of the Hotel Akron, one of the finest hotels in Prague, he got into conversation with an older gentleman in whom he confided his innermost wish: to marry into a wealthy family. Actually, he did more than just confide his dream—he brought it down to earth by asking the stranger if he knew such a family. The gentleman, whose name was Herr Fried, was an eminent lawyer, whose tall and distinguished appearance was marred by a clubfoot he had had since birth. He had never married. In many a royal court throughout history, certain persons marred by a deformity, such as dwarfs or eunuchs, became confidants of royalty. In the case of Herr Fried, he won the confidence of the "House of Brach" and was free to come and go there. In addition, he was a particular favorite of my grandmother, *Oma* Luise, who enjoyed, it is said, having intellectual conversations with him. From this favored position, Herr Fried knew the family well. He knew the business side which my grandfather readily discussed with him and he also knew the family side, as shared with him by my grandmother.

One of her concerns at the time was her two daughters, aged twenty-two and twenty-four, who were as different from each other as night and day. Erna, the oldest, had flaming red hair and a nature to match. In spite of the most carefully chaperoned upbringing, she had managed at seventeen to have an affair with her second cousin, Paul. This young man, whose father was a cousin of my grandfather, lived with his brother in an apartment above a newspaper and tobacco shop in Olomouc. Her frequent unchaperoned visits to the apartment upstairs were observed by the shopkeeper's wife, who reported them to her family. Whereupon Erna, at age eighteen, was forced by my grandfather to marry Paul. The incident was a scandal and, even as a married woman, her reputation was marred in the eyes of the family Brach forever.

My mother, Helene, whose hair was brown, seemed by contrast like a butterfly still in its cocoon. Her complete lack of interest in the opposite sex was beginning to concern her parents.

It seems that both versions of how my father met my mother are true. My father's family side, that an ad had appeared in the *Frankfurter Zeitung,* no doubt is true. So is my mother's side, that my father had met Herr Fried in the Hotel Akron in Prague, with one small difference: the meeting was not accidental. It had been arranged by my grandfather, following my father's reply to the ad. The former had sent Herr Fried as his emissary to check out the candidate.

Herr Fried obviously approved of the young man who, having passed muster, was sent on to meet the family.

Leonard Brach remained in Dresden to tend to the affairs of the malt business but sent his wife Luise, his daughter Helene, his son Fredie, his niece Susie, and a young friend of Susie's, to vacation at the Hotel Berghof in Spindlermühle, a resort in the German-speaking region of Czechoslovakia. When Arthur Hahn, with modest means but high hopes and a huge suitcase arrived, he checked into a farmhouse that offered accommodations upstairs for himself and downstairs for cattle.

Young Arthur had taken along the huge wardrobe trunk filled with clothes, for he wanted to make the best possible impression. The trunk, which had to be carried up the wooden steps by two farmhands, opened vertically, like two doors connected with brass hinges. One side contained gray canvas-covered shelves for shirts, shoes and underwear. The other side was like a traveling closet for hanging suits full-length. He had arrived, in other words, like an actor on tour, with a wardrobe full of costumes ready for any part he needed to play.

After the trunk was securely established in his small room and its hinges opened to let in some air, Arthur Hahn gave careful thought to his next move. Neither money nor time allowed for any dilly-dallying. He had asked for a seven-day leave from his job at the bank, which his strict father/employer had grudgingly granted. Certainly he, Jakob Hahn, had no need to travel into the *Ausland*, why then should his son? The small wage he was paid by his father left no leeway to stay beyond the allotted week. All that had to be accomplished would have to be done within that stretch of time.

From his window, Arthur Hahn could clearly see the Hotel Berghof where the family he had come to meet was staying. They had gone so far as to send their emissary, Herr Fried, to meet him and check him out in Prague, and he had allowed Arthur to approach closer. Now what was he to do? No messenger was sent to his farmhouse inn to invite him to join the family for tea or anything. As a matter of fact, he wasn't even sure they knew he had arrived.

As he gazed out his window, the Hotel Berghof looked more and more like a castle to him, and he, the young knight, had to ford the moat, slay the dragon, gain entry, and ask for the hand of the young damsel. Arthur Hahn felt ready for the task.

First off, he decided that he would take his main meals at the hotel; the farmhouse only served breakfast anyway. Having made that decision, he freshened up, changed his clothes and walked purposefully to the hotel. There he left his card at the desk and penned a note which said that he brought regards from a mutual friend, Herr Fried, and expressed the hope he would have the pleasure of meeting the esteemed family Brach, of whom he had heard so much. Then he went to the dining room and after inquiring exactly where the family Brach sat, requested a table in close proximity to them.

Arthur Hahn was already at table when the Brachs arrived. The note had reached Luise Brach in the course of the afternoon, but how many of the others knew about it is not clear. Certainly,

Helene was entirely unaware of it. But when the new guest raised his Stein of beer toward them in a silent toast, Fredie told them not to look in his direction and intimated he was an imposter. Young Fredie, the only male at the Brach table, took a dislike to young Arthur on sight and refused to toast him back.

This slight, however, did not deter the young knight. It served rather to clarify his approach which had now to be directed first toward Luise Brach, the mother.

Arthur Hahn, who adored his own mother, Julia, and who was secure in the knowledge of being her favorite, felt on firm footing with all mothers and, in fact, with the female gender in general.

No one seems to remember exactly how it all happened, but Luise Brach, the matron at the table of five, did not reject the immaculately dressed young man who clicked his heels and bowed like the Prince of Prussia when he kissed her hand. If her dear friend Walter Fried had sent him, she would allow him to accompany her on the daily walks she took with her daughter, her son, her niece and her niece's friend.

Nature walks were the main activity in Spindlermühle. There were morning walks in woods and fields, afternoon walks, and short evening promenades in front of the hotel. Occasionally, guests decided to make an expedition, which meant to climb a nearby mountain. Such a decision was never made without letting the hotel know the night before so as to alert the kitchen to their absence at the midday meal and have a substantial lunch packed instead. How many thousands of photographs have been taken of European families sitting on rocks near streams munching picnic lunches?

While accompanying Luise Brach and her children on that first walk, it was established that Arthur Hahn was not living in the hotel, as had of course been assumed, but that he was staying at a farmhouse in the village below—a fact which was immediately used against him by Fredie. It was perfect proof, he said, that this fellow with the fancy clothes and the Germanic airs was a *Heiratsschwindler*, a person who was out to marry for money. Fredie lost no time pointing out the farmhouse, which the girls could see from their hotel balcony, including the cow which just then walked out of the downstairs door and started grazing. They all shrieked with derisive laughter, including Helene. It was just too funny, they thought, that this fancy fellow lived with a cow.

But Luise Brach thought differently and made it her business to call on the young man to get a closer look. She returned from this visit highly impressed. He was neat as a pin, she said; a fact which probably did not impress any of the other four. Still, when Luise Brach stood on the hotel balcony and saw the farmhouse inn below she ignored the grazing cow, but gazed approvingly at the young German's pants which hung near the open window in order to insure a perfect crease. That, to her, was the deciding factor.

If consuming whipped cream and Viennese chocolates were Austrian foibles of the time, Luise Brach was not a typical Austrian lady. She inclined rather to birchwater and cucumbers. The birchwater she used to massage her scalp and freshen her naturally wavy hair; the cucumbers she served with tomatoes and radishes for simple suppers. She did not believe in eating heavy meals before retiring and initiated a kind of *nouvelle cuisine* in her Czech/Austrian kitchen—unthickened soups and sauces, fresh fruits more often than sweet desserts—all this long before people everywhere became health and diet conscious. She was a Spartan and although she certainly had the means, allowed herself no indulgences. Neat, clean and practical were some of the epithets she applied to herself. Reading newspapers rather than romantic novels kept her abreast of political affairs. During the War she had served as a volunteer for the Red Cross, dressing the wounds of soldiers in hospitals.

Neat and clean and practical—interested in newspapers rather than books—these traits also described the young man who lived in the farmhouse inn below. Luise Brach could share with him more than with her own son, Fredie, who increasingly gave indications of being a typical rich man's son—taking things for granted, talking more than doing. Although she had at first accepted the young stranger because he had been sent by her friend, she now endorsed him herself, allowing him to accompany them on their group walks, and also to walk alone with Helene.

Helene Brach was twenty-two years old when the young German walked at her side. When she momentarily stumbled over a branch that had fallen across her path, her companion seized her in his arms and, lifting her over the obstruction, declared fervently, "That's how I want to carry you through life!" The declaration startled Helene. Knowing nothing about the ad in the paper or the meeting with Herr Fried at the Hotel Akron, she found the young man's ardor out of keeping. Very few people had entered her life, and Helene Brach lacked experience in judging others. She knew she had to listen to her parents and her governesses and to think on her own as little as possible. Her sister Erna had set a bad example of what could happen when one broke loose. "She danced out of line," they said of her and made her pay dearly for it, deeming her a fallen woman throughout her life.

Actually, Helene had once cut out on her own too, and this act of self-assertion had not ended well either. When she was sixteen, she was allowed to go to a social dancing class which was attended by the young men and women of Olomouc society. Each week she was brought there either by her mother, or her aunt Ida. Without being particularly interested in any of the young men, Helene went through the steps of Polonaise, the Quadrille and other social dances dating back to the gilded age of Kaiser

Franz Josef, to the time of the Austro-Hungarian Empire, which everyone still referred to nostalgically and which had set the tone for social etiquette, though it was originally borrowed from France.

Toward the end of the year, the dancing school had a formal ball which was a major event, of course, for the young social set. On the day of the ball, Helene's white dress trimmed with pink satin, lay perfectly pressed on her bed. It had been hand-sewn for her by two dressmaker sisters. The cook had finished baking two dozen gingerbread hearts, decorating them with ribbons. White frosting lettered the name of each boy. These were favors which the young men would pin on their lapels.

By early afternoon all was in readiness and Helene, as was often the case, had nothing to do. A sudden desire to have a manicure seized her and she went to her mother's room to ask permission to go into town. Her mother, who was reading a newspaper, did not think that a manicure was necessary and told her to stay home. But Helene's restlessness grew and she came into her mother's room repeatedly in the hope that she would change her mind. Finally, Helene took off on her own, hurrying to the Littauer Strasse, the main street in downtown Olomouce. It wasn't far, but she had not realized that it was the Saturday before Christmas and the manicurist was busy. Having made no appointment, she had to wait a long time. By the time she returned home, it was quite late. She rushed into her room and saw that the dress that had been lying on her bed like an innocent white bud had disappeared. She ran to her mother and asked, "Where is my dress?" "In the fire," said Luise Brach. "In the fire." Then Helene ran into the kitchen but the gingerbread hearts were also gone. "Where are the hearts?" she asked. "In the fire too" was the heartless reply.

Almost seven years had passed since this incident, seven years during which little had happened in Helene's life. She studied French and played the piano, but in the main she was Snow White, quietly asleep.

The walks with young Arthur, however, were having a decided effect on her. Color appeared in her cheeks and she became noticeably animated—so much so, that Luise Brach telephoned her husband and asked him to come quickly and meet the young man before his return to Germany.

When Leonard Brach arrived, things proceeded at even greater speed. Before anyone could fully grasp it, there was talk of announcing a formal engagement on Helene's birthday in September. But that was a full two months away and too long to wait. Finally it was decided that the family Brach would pay a formal visit to the family Hahn in Bad Hersfeld in mid-August, exactly within one month.

Just before leaving, Arthur Hahn, who had stayed three days beyond his allotted seven, took Helene to the local photographer and had a picture taken, as proof back home that all was true and not a fairy tale.

The knight had forded the moat, scaled the walls of the castle, and been granted the hand of the damsel.

In geology, a fault is a break in rock strata that causes a section to become dislocated along the line of the fracture. In the case of the German-speaking peoples, such a "fault" or social fracture occurred hundreds of years ago, when one area remained closely tied to the Holy Roman Empire under the Hapsburgs, and the other, under the Hohenzollerns, produced the Reformation and Protestantism, and gave rise to Prussia. In this latter region, Germany proper, a large middle class was formed due to the influence of industrialization, public education, and the work ethic.

The Brachs, on the other hand, though having moved into

Germany proper from the other German-speaking region, were in their ways still living in the Austria they had known. There, the courtly days of Paris and Vienna had had a prolonged social influence, with members of the aristocracy, wealthy merchants, intellectuals, and artists on the one side of the social spectrum and poorly educated laborers and servants on the other.

To the Brachs, the Hahns, though certainly above average in their small German-Jewish community, were nevertheless decidedly *bourgeois*.

To the female members of the Hahn family, however, the Brachs seemed to have been sent from heaven. Only good could come from such a contact, they felt, and the possibility of becoming actually related to these princes was almost beyond belief. Arthur's sister, Bertie, lost no time in fantasizing introductions to a long line of wealthy men, one of whom she would eventually marry (but not before attending scores of balls and gala affairs and breaking the hearts of dozens of suitors).

Mother Julia saw herself visiting her successful son in Dresden or Berlin, where "the new life" she could only read about as she spread newspapers under rumps of geese and chickens was taking place. How to get the house ready? What to serve? What to wear? Who would sit next to whom? Was the table large enough?

The two brothers, Isfried and Rudi, also imagined that this social expansion would benefit them. And, if they harbored any envy of Arthur (after all it was he who had fallen into this "butter tub"), they also knew that neither of them could have performed likewise. Isfried was too simple and honest. Rudi was too easygoing. It took a special combination of ambitious shrewdness and charisma that was typically Arthur's nature, not theirs.

No one in the Brach family observed the Sabbath, but Leonard Brach took into expedient consideration the fact that his arrival on a Saturday, though convenient for himself, would be unforgivable to the orthodox Jakob Hahn. The Brachs, therefore, got off the train a stop before Bad Hersfeld, respectfully stayed overnight in a small hotel, and continued their journey on Sunday morning. They were met at the station by Isfried, the eldest son, who carried a bouquet of long-stemmed red roses for Luise Brach. Then, moving on foot through town, the retinue which included luggage-carrying redcaps, was met in front of the town hall by Rudi, the youngest son, who also carried a bouquet of flowers as a sign of welcome. Arthur, who had stage-managed the Brachs' arrival by directing his brothers to position themselves at strategic points with flowers, awaited the family at the front door of his parents' house with a bouquet for Helene.

Upstairs, excitement and nervous energy ran rampant. A welcome and immediate distraction from any awkward moments (experienced particularly by Julia Hahn, who generally found it easier to shed a tear than to speak; or by the not so socially deft Isfried and Rudi) was overcome by busyness. Julia had to apply last minute touches to meat, fish and fowl, and the two brothers were winding up the victrola so that it continually played the latest hit song from the Berlin cabarets; a song appropriately called: *Ach, wie ich die Lene liebe*, (Oh, how I love Helene).

It was sung by a raspy-voiced Lotte-Lenya/Marlene-Dietrich-type called Claire Waldorff and began like this:

Ach, wie ich die Lene liebe, Ha, Ha, Ha.
Ach, ich fühle mächt'ge Triebe, Ha, Ha, Ha.
Oh, how I love Helene, Ha. Ha. Ha.
Oh, I have such powerful feelings. Ha. Ha. Ha.

No longer Vienna, but Berlin; the Berlin of the 1920s with its neo-expressionist influences was the latest fashion. Not a Viennese waltz and a society which still modeled itself on the Napoleonic court, but satire sung by low-slung, unprotected and daring women—new messages leaking out of underground cabarets at four in the morning and wafting smoke-like into the homes even of small-town people.

Hats were worn askew.

They were ten at table. Jakob Hahn and Julia Hahn took their appointed seats. He farthest from, she closest to the kitchen. Luise B. was the table partner of Jakob H. Leonard B. was the table partner of Julia H. Dark-haired, dark-eyed Bertie, already vigorously flirting with blond, blue-eyed Fredie, was seated next to him, of course. Arthur sat next to Helene and his two brothers squeezed into any available space as best they could. Erna, already six years married, was not present.

Now it was Father Jakob's turn. Wearing a black silk yamulka, he stood over the *Challe*, the Jewish loaf, which lay covered with a silken cloth on a porcelain platter. Holding his hands over the loaf, he pronounced the *brocho*: "boruch ato hascham elohenu melech hoaulom hamauzeh lechem min hoorez." (Blessed are thou, oḥ Lord, King of the universe, who bringest forth bread from the earth.)

All heads were for that moment respectfully bowed. Felt hats, though not askew, were on the heads of Leonard B. and Fredie B., who did not have yamulkas. Fredie, always unserious, saw the whole thing as a joke. As a matter of fact, he had laid plans to extricate himself and shorten his required presence by requesting that Lisa Arnhold, the ailing wife of eminent banker Heinrich Arnhold, head of the Dresdner Bank, place an urgent call on the pretext that she lay dying and had to speak with him immediately, and in person, on behalf of Paula her adopted daughter, whom Fredie was courting.

Whether Fredie actually received such a call, or whether he just said he did, is not clear. But either way, he was permitted to return to Dresden almost immediately. He did marry Paula, though the marriage ended in divorce. And as far as the Arnholds are concerned, they soon joined forces with the remaining partners of the House of S. Bleichroeder, founding first in London and then in New York a prospering new firm under the name of Arnhold and S. Bleichroeder.

But for the time being, dinner was served.

Between courses which were served by a waiter in white gloves—Julia's idea to lend elegance to the occasion—everyone knew that one thing remained to be settled: the dowry.

In Jewish it is called "talking *takhles*." In America one speaks of getting down to "brass tacks," or "talking turkey." Surely every country and every language has a saying for that moment, when everything is stripped down to the bare bones and a deal is struck.

The two principals, Leonard B. and Jakob H., one clean-shaven, the other wearing a Kaiser Wilhelm mustache that protruded from each side of his face like the horns of an extinct breed of wild bison, knew what still had to be done and how to do it. Dark-suited, with gold watch chains across their vested chests, they arose after dinner to take a walk.

Helene and Arthur trailed behind them out of earshot; Fredie bid his adieus and caught a train back to Dresden; Bertie returned to her room with a violent migraine headache; and everyone was in need of a rest.

Four hours later, they reassembled. The two patriarchs were relaxed and amiable. Things had gone well. They took their seats at the dining table. Jakob H. rose to speak.

Arthur and Helene are good children, he said. They had

found each other and he saw no reason to stand in their way. Arthur would make a good husband and a worthy son-in-law to Helene's esteemed father, whose business he would enter and for whom he would work and do his best to make things prosper. "All is in good order and I have no objection to any of this," he continued, "except for one thing."

All eyes were upon him.

"What about Kosher?" he asked. "Who would keep a Kosher kitchen? Without the assurance that my son's household will uphold the Jewish dietary traditions, I cannot give my complete consent."

Silence. Bertie's migraine was throbbing. Julia's rosy country cheeks paled. The obstacle was real. Could it be solved?

"Liesl can do the Kosher cooking," Julia offered suddenly. "I will send her to Dresden to live with Arthur and Helene."

Liesl had served in the Hahn household for more than twenty years. She had come from the Schwalm, the surrounding countryside where the villages still had thatched roofs for storks to nest in the spring, and no plumbing. Liesl had come into the Hahn household as a young girl and although she was not Jewish, she had been trained by Julia in all the details of keeping a Kosher kitchen. She was the solution.

Thereupon, Jakob H. dropped a glass to the floor, stepped on it and said "Good luck."

Bertie fainted.

In February 1926, the bride and groom walked under an arch of sabers held aloft by the Veda fraternity brothers in the grand Dresden town house of Leonard and Luise Brach. And Liesl, clutching a huge goosedown pillow, her prized possession, came to the big city to keep the Kosher kitchen for Helene.

I was born barely a year later, having been conceived during my parent's honeymoon on the French Riviera.

When, upon her return to Dresden, my mother learned of her condition, she started to sob. "But why are you crying, young woman?" the doctor asked. "You are married, aren't you?'

That was clearly not the point. Motherhood was not what my mother had expected from marriage. Not so soon. Not yet. More than anything else, she had hoped that marriage would allow her to be carefree and gay. To do as she pleased and to finally "go to the ball."

The *Elbschloss Malzfabrik*, the "Castle-on-the-Elbe Malthouse," for which Leonard Brach needed a German son-in-law, did not squat in a field of poppies in the east European grainbelt, as did its Moravian sistership. Rather, it practically leaned against the strangely shaped sandstone rocks for which Schöna, near Dresden, was known. Shaded also by dark green trees, vines and ferns, this river fortress emanated the dank smell of fermentation which fosters the growth of mushrooms, moss and the making of beer. The malthouse was built so close to the river's edge that a loading dock and a narrow railroad siding were just about all there was room for in front.

Barley, the basic grain used for the preparation of the malt for beer, was shipped by boat from Czechoslovakia. Tons and tons of golden kernels traveled slowly on the river Elbe to the malthouse. There, the grain was soaked in water, dried and made to sprout according to a secret family formula. The processed malt was then loaded onto railroad cars and shipped to breweries all over Germany. The new son-in-law's task was to woo the German brewers to buy their malt from the newly established branch.

Originally, Leonard Brach had in mind a different task for my father. After the "Hersfeld Agreement," he had sent him to a school in Berlin to learn the chemical preparation of grain, in order to be in charge of the malt laboratory. But my father had shown no aptitude for the scientific side of the business. His great

Brief-Adresse:
HERMANN BRACH
Olomouc 2.
Telegramm-Adresse:
BRACH OLOMOUC
Postsparkassakonto
Praha Nr. 5076
TELEFON Nr. 11

Hanna - Malzfabriken
Hermann Brach Olmütz

CODES:
A B.C. Code 5th Edition „Improved"
A B C Code 6th Edition
Rudolf Mosse Code
Staudt & Hundius
A B.C. 5th Edition

Fabrik in Olomouc — Elbschloß-Malzfabrik in Schöna a. Elbe.

Exportmarke AURORA

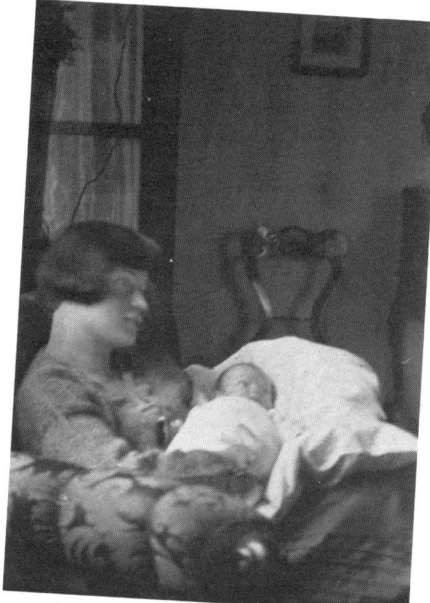

Left:
Opa Brach, *Oma* Luise in Meran, 1920
Above:
My mother and newborn Hannelore with Biedermeier chair in background
Upper right:
The *Familien Haus* in Olomouc, Moravia
My mother with her parents, circa 1920
Lower right:
Night before the wedding. Dinner party in the *Salon* at Bergstrasse Number 16.
Left to Right, first row:
Opa Brach, *Oma* Luise, my mother Helene, my father Arthur, *Oma* Julia, *Opa* Jakob
Left to Right, second row:
uncle Robert, aunt Erna, uncle Willie, aunt Ida, aunt Bertie, uncle Paul, Herr Fried, uncle Fredie
Foreground sitting on floor: aunt Susie

flair was clearly salesmanship.

Bergstrasse Number 16 was the house my father went to every morning. Up the marble-faced entrance foyer, up the carpeted stairway flanked by pots of fresh azaleas, or tulips, or whatever was in season; up to the second storey, whose floors were so well polished that one had to be careful not to fall. There, the *Elbschloss Malzfabrik* had its home office. And there, in a suite of rooms, secretaries with corkscrew curls typed letters on clanky manual typewriters, and bookkeepers, wearing green visors to shade their eyes from the glare of electric bulbs, made careful entries in heavy ledgers.

There, too, at approximately 10:30 each morning, uncle Fredie snuck downstairs into the kitchen for a midmorning snack, or *Gabelfrühstück*. He was a *Nascher*, an in-between eater, who usually helped himself to slices of rye bread and fresh goose fat in which, hopefully, some liver slices lay buried.

There, *Opa* Brach as I called my grandfather, walked with my father up and down garden paths richly strewn with white gravel, the *Kieselsteine*, that made a crunchy sound beneath their steady steps. *Opa* Brach liked to talk business while walking. Hands folded behind his back, he strode in his park-like garden with my father and other lieutenants, like a head of state. Definitely the man in charge.

There, *Oma* Luise as I called my grandmother, sat in the *Wintergarten*, the glass-enclosed veranda, surrounded by palms, cacti, rubber trees and other botanic specimens native to more southern climes, embroidering a pillowslip and talking to my mother about servants. To *Oma* Luise, servants were not a status symbol, but an essential crew for the maintenance of property at its optimum perfection. Actually, *Oma* Luise could do any of the individual tasks herself. She could cook, bake, clean and polish as well as any of her servants. That made her an excellent overseer and she imbued her position with as much efficiency as if she were running trains. If, on the second floor, *Opa* Brach was in charge of business, *Oma* Brach, on the first floor, was definitely in charge of everything else including the well-being of her husband, the head of state.

Oma Luise was tall and slim, which was unusual for our family's Austrian/German stock. Most of the ladies of my family were short and well rounded.

Two small diamonds nestled in her pierced ears. She wore no other jewelry, except for a diamond hairclip and chose "sparrow colors"—greys, browns and an occasional pale blue—for her tailored clothing. Makeup never touched her lips and her clothing was "English." That's what tailored tweed suits and silk shirts buttoned to the neck were called. Her hats were never decorated with veils, feathers or flowers, but were mannish felts, and once in a while she even wore a *Schlips*, a kind of man's tie.

Her parquet floors were blond and gleaming. Her Persian rugs were *ausgeklopft*, that is, beaten in the backyard, perferably in the snow. Her chandeliers were regularly dismantled and dipped in warm suds. Walls were wiped with still warm, freshly baked bread which erased stains and absorbed dust. Her dining room was Chippendale. Her chinaware was hand-painted Meissen complete for fifty; it included a stunning soup tureen large enough for baptising a baby.

Her salon/music room was bathed in yellow; its golden hues were interrupted only by a large, black Steinway grand. Mealtimes were always announced by striking a muted brass gong and calling in French, "à table, à table." Apples were never bitten into, but served on fruit plates or sectioned, *trangiert*, with mother-of-pearl-handled fruit knives and forks. This was woman's work, done at the table. Men never peeled or cut their own fruit. *Opa* Brach favored a certain apple, the *Calville*. It arrived from Merano, Italy, in wooden crates at certain seasons.

A born administrator at a time when administration for a woman could hardly go beyond her home, *Oma* Luise ran her household as if it were an official estate ready to receive important dignitaries from around the world. Actually, no one like that ever

...ergstrasse Number 16:

...ockwise from top right:
...itrine with Meissen china
...y father striding pruposefully. Dresden, circa 1926
...ergstrasse Number 16
... e *Wintergarten*
... e *Salon*

came to Bergstrasse Number 16. All activities, business and social, involved relatives only. If my grandparents wielded great influence, it did not go beyond family. Of course, I did not realize that at the time. To me, *Opa* and *Oma* Brach were like a king and queen, and Bergstrasse Number 16 was a great seat of power. Everything seemed to me to be happening there. Nothing happened anywhere else.

My parents took a large apartment within walking distance of Bergstrasse Number 16. There Liesl continued to wear her traditional many-petticoated regional costume, her white stockings and the peculiar bun-like cap worn by the *Schwelmerinnen*, the women of Schwalm. Oblivious to her new surroundings and circumstances, she also continued to call my father, whom she had known since he was a little boy, by his first name. This irritated him. He now wanted to be addressed as Dr. Hahn and he asked her also to please use the more formal *Sie* rather than the informal *du* when addressing him. But Liesl would not change her ways. She refused to call him "Dr. Hahn," and he would tolerate nothing less. One day, Liesl took her goose-down pillow and said she wanted to go back home. No one detained her.

So much for Kosher.

While I played in the sandbox in my grandparents' garden with my cousins Peter, Gitty, Ellen, Bobbie and Renate, National Socialism under Hitler took over.

My cousin Peter, who was the oldest and went to the *Gymnasium*, brought back to us, in the garden, a song he had learned from his classmates in school. It went like this:

Axelbaum mach die Türen auf,
Hitler kommt im Dauerlauf.
Muss sich eine Zelle mieten,
Weil bei ihm die Vöglein piepen.

Translation:

Axelbaum (the local insane asylum), open your doors,
Hitler comes a'running.
He has to rent a cell for himself,
Because there are birdies chirping in his head.

Peter and his classmates accompanied this song with a finger-play. The scenario went like this:

Axelbaum, open your doors.
(Open lid of inkwell)
Hitler comes a'running.
(Run finger along desk towards inkwell).
He has to rent a cell for himself,
(Pretend to stick finger in inkwell).
Because there are birdies chirping in his head.
(Close inkwell fast. Hitler is caught in inkwell.)

Naturally, Peter taught this to all of us, his much younger cousins. We were greatly impressed with what the big boys were up to in the *Gymnasium* and sing-songed the verse in the sandbox at Bergstrasse Number 16, making a hole in the sand, imagining Hitler jumping inside, and quickly closing it up so he would never, never get out.

One day, when I had the mumps, my parents came into my room with a stranger carrying a briefcase. The stranger sat down near my bed and said he'd like to ask me a few questions. I looked at my parents. They stood stiff and tense and said nothing.

Had I ever heard a song, the stranger wanted to know, which went like this:

Axelbaum mach die Türen auf,
Hitler kommt im Dauerlauf.
Muss sich eine Zelle mieten,
Weil beim ihm Vöglein piepen.

Yes, I had.

Where had I heard it, the stranger wanted to know.
I sang it in my grandparents' garden.
   Who taught it to you?
My cousin.
   What is his name?
His name is Peter.
   How old is he?
Thirteen.
   Danke schön.

The man left with my parents to go to Peter's house, but Peter wasn't there. He was in the park looking for chestnuts. They found him there. Then Peter, and his bag full of chestnuts, and his parents and mine were taken to the police station. There Peter was asked for the names of his classmates who had sung the song with him and especially for the name of the boy who had introduced the song to the others. Both sets of parents were warned that they would be held responsible for any future acts against the Führer on the part of their children and the case was recorded.

For the time being, that was all.

Herr Vogel, the bookkeeper with the green visor at Bergstrasse Number 16, had magnificent penmanship. He could script ordinary words to make them look like wedding invitations, or condolences, as the case might be.

It was Herr Vogel, the scribe, who had informed the *Geheimpolizei*, the Gestapo. He had heard us singing in the garden.

In the apartment house where I lived with my parents (and where it happened that the German Expressionist painter, Otto Dix, also lived), I played occasionally with Günther, the superintendant's son. We would meet in the yard. There we would dig for coins. These coins, which were not too hard to find, were made of lightweight, cheap metal and completely worthless. Minted during the German inflation which followed World War I, they had simply been thrown out. Still, to us, finding the money was exciting. Perhaps, looking for these lightweight coins—history buried in loam—was not unlike searching for Indian arrowheads in an American backyard. Except for the fact that the time of the American Indian was much longer ago. The German inflation had occurred only a few years before Günther and I were born.

When you are a child, any time before your birth is long ago. "The olden days." It is hard for a child to comprehend the past and, also, the future. It lives completely in the now, the present. And the present for me, those first few years in Dresden, was very fine indeed.

But once in awhile, something "buried in loam" would rear its head. Then something would change and never be the same again.

Clockwise from upper right:
Sitting with my cousins, left to right: Gitty, Peter Bobbie and I
Standing in the garden with my cousins Ellen and Gitty. I am in the middle
Hannelore standing on the garden bridge with hedge roses
Hannelore with cornucopia presented on first day of school
Hannelore standing with neighbors Gunther and the two sons of painter Otto Dix
The Synogogue in Dresden. Jewish School building on left
Public School, first grade, Dresden 1932. I am in the middle, front row

Such a rearing up occurred when I was seven years old. My father announced that I would have to change schools. He said Jewish children could no longer attend public schools and I would have to go to the Jewish school downtown.

My first day of public school only a year before had been a happy occasion. All of us in first grade had received a gift from the Board of Education. It was a colorful paper cornucopia filled with candy, new pencils, erasers, penholders and crayons. Herr Jakobowski, our teacher, had passed them out—fresh tools with which to learn about the world. We were all six years old and eager.

On my way to school during that first year, I often heard the thumping beat of history. Swastikas were everywhere, brown-shirted men goose-stepping—black boots, black belts, black leather straps diagonally across their chests, iron helmets, right arms raised. What a show of unity! What a show of strength! It was exciting in a goose-pimply, heart-thumping way.

The thumping beat of history about to be born.

It came as a shock to me to have to change schools.

Why? I asked.

Because we are Jewish, was my father's reply.

Is being Jewish something bad?

And when the street car conductor who saw me every morning getting off in the old part of town, with my schoolbag, wished to know the name of my school, I blanched and did not know what to say. I could not tell him.

Fear.

During this period we drove more and more to Czechoslovakia to spend our weekends. There we would gorge on *Karlbader Oblaten*, the wafer-thin sweet waffles freshly pressed at the Karlsbad spa. Also on goose livers. These were golden-hued and so soft that they spread like butter on a good piece of sour rye. Czech geese were force-fed to produce abnormally large livers, a procedure which was not allowed in Germany, a nation which credited itself to be more humane and civilized.

In Czechoslovakia on holiday, we were not unlike geese ourselves, stuffing ourselves at country inns, then waddling into forests permeated by the intoxicating fragrance of mushrooms. By mid-afternoon, we were at it again, ready for *Kaffee* and *Kuchen*, or another round of *Palachinken*, the thin rolled pancakes filled with fresh strawberry or apricot marmalade.

From the way we acted on these holidays, no one could have guessed how much we dreaded the border crossings. First, on the German side, the be-swastikaed guards would check our passports, register the license number of our car and ask if we were taking any valuables out of the country, to which my parents always replied, "No." When the guards snapped, "Heil Hitler!" and flashed the Nazi salute, we knew the examination was over.

We also knew that we were expected to salute back. "Heil Hitler!" had become the hello, the goodbye, the please, the thank you, the I'm O.K./you're O.K., the overall password of the German language. If one did not say it one could not "pass."

Stitterich would silently salute for us and then cautiously drive on. Thank God for that. None of us could have raised our hands or uttered that phrase. Still, that moment of crossing the border cried out for a counter ritual. If we had been Catholic, the sign of the cross might have helped to mitigate the fury and the fear.

The Czech border guards were much more informal. One might almost say they were glad to see us. German tourists were good spenders and the country, which had become a nation less than two decades before, needed currency. Once in a while a particularly relaxed guard wouldn't even stop the car, just wave us on. Of course, Stitterich always stopped for a moment anyway. After all, this was *die Grenze*, the border. If they were too lazy, or too far into their bottle of Schnapps, too bad. He, at least, knew how to conduct himself upon crossing from one nation to another. And anyway, how would it look if he would just speed past? Suspicious, to say the least.

I guess he was right.

But coming back was different. At the German station, all the adults in our car always had to disrobe. The men were taken to one part of the building, the ladies to another. While this went on I would sit alone in the empty car. Nothing moved. Even the air was standing still.

Then, when it was over, we would drive on in silence. Everyone was depressed. If anyone spoke it was mainly to compare notes on how he or she was treated. My mother might say that this time she had a dreadful woman, who made her take everything off. Or my father might remark that the one he had this time was a little better than the week before.

But, usually, things got worse, not better.

I did not know until many years later that the true purpose of these Czechoslovakian weekends was not walking in the woods, picking mushrooms and eating liver dumplings in country inns. It was the transferral of funds into foreign bank accounts. Each trip meant a deposit.

No one can tell me now just how this was done when we crossed the border in our automobile. Where was the money stashed? It always had to be cash or other tangible valuables like gold and jewelry. But whichever way, and unbeknownst to my mother and me, this was the true reason for our Czechoslovakian holidays during the years between 1934 and 1937.

There were other ways too. One emanated directly from the *Elbschloss Malzfabrik* in Schöna. There, every Friday Herr Kahn, our plant manager, would leave his river fortress and ford the Elbe via ferry to Herrensgretschen, a small Czech ferry station nestled in a narrow opening of rocks and trees on the other side of the river, to drink a glass of beer with a "friend." Between sips of *Pilsner Urquell* a weekly transaction took place.

But the most daring scheme and the one which managed to take most of the money out of the country, was based on a loophole in a German directive on travel into foreign countries and amounts of money that could be spent there. With a doctor's certificate prescribing a Swiss sanitarium as a cure, German citizens during the years of 1936 and 1937 were allowed to leave the country for health reasons and to take with them several thousand German Marks, which without the health certificate they would not have been able to do. Here is where my father's legal training really paid off, for he masterminded an "underground railroad" where close to a thousand persons, relatives, friends, and friends of friends got themselves to Switzerland for "health reasons." He would pay their way in Germany and they, in turn, would deposit the money, which they were legally allowed to take out of the country but did not have to use, with a Herr Lear in Switzerland. Ernst Lear was the owner of the Waldrand Hotel in Kandersteg, in the Berner Oberland, the German-speaking part of Switzerland.

We vacationed there every summer. The chalet-style hotel looked like a pretty toy. Red geraniums dotted the wooden balconies facing green meadows. Behind the hotel was a high cliff from which a white waterfall continuously poured into an ice-cold mountain stream stocked with trout. Near the stream the Boy Scouts had their international camp. Picking field flowers in the rich meadow of the hotel, I had no idea about the real reason we always came there. The Waldrand Hotel, my father would say, was his favorite vacation place.

Fresh salmon was served there on silver platters by young, attractive waitresses in black dresses and white lace-edged aprons. My father was always in a good mood when we were there.

Kandersteg, Switzerland:

Clockwise from upper right:
My father was always in a good mood there.
Uncle Fredie standing with aunt Bertie in front of his white convertible
uncle Robert, aunt Steffi, cousin Ellen, my mother, Hannelore, uncle Eric, uncle Fredie
Hannelore and cousin Ellen with butterfly nets
Isolde Elber and I
My father climbing the Alps
Isolde Elber and I
Hannelore in the rich meadow next to the Waldrand Hotel

In 1936 I had pneumonia. Everybody was worried. My father brought me *Brüssler Trauben,* blue grapes imported from Brussels. Whenever someone was ill, it was thought that these dark, luscious grapes would be good for him or her.

After I was well enough to be up and about, it was suggested that I should go to Switzerland with my mother for complete recuperation. As an added treat, my parents said I could take with me any friend I chose. It was a hard choice. My best friends from school where Isolde Elber and Elfriede Kaimsky. Elfriede didn't have a father and her mother worked as a maid. Isolde was an excellent student and very good in sports. I finally settled on Isolde. After all, it was winter and we would ski.

Where is Islode Elber now? and Elfriede Kaimsky?
Where is Wera Bernstein, who wrote in my diary the following thought:

> Dein Leben sei fröhlich and heiter
> Kein Leiden betrübe Dein Herz
> Das Glück sei stehts Dein Begleiter
> Nie treffe dich Kummer und Schmerz.

Translation
> May your life always be happy and gay
> May no sorrow cloud your heart
> May luck always be your companion
> And may you never experience unhappiness and pain.

Where is Friedel Winkler, who wrote the same verse, because she copied it from Wera?

Where is Yvonne Stern, who wrote:

The world turns
So does human fortune
Enjoy happiness
It does not return
Bear unhappiness
With a pleasant attitude
Just look, it changes, too
And all will be well.

And where is Ruth Halpern, who quoted Goethe in my book?

There is nothing more unique
And attractive about man
Than that he can trust
And be trusted.

And where is Zilla Roth, who wrote:

If you are clever and rich
Do good deeds with it
And do not say
You must first be more clever and still richer.

Dein Leben sei fröhlich und heiter
Kein Leiden betrübe Dein Herz,
Das Glück sei stets Dein Begleiter
Nie treffe Dich Kummer und Schmerz.

Dies schrieb Dir
Deine Freundin
Wera Bernstein.

Den 17.2.1937

Frl. ......

Es dreht sich die Welt
Und der Menschen Geschick,
Genieße die Freude
Sie kehrt nicht zurück!
Das Üble ertragen
Mit fröhlichem Mut
Denn sehe es dreht sich
Und wird wieder gut.

......freundlichen Erinner-
ung

Was frag ich viel nach Geld und Gut,
Wenn ich zufrieden bin,
Gibt Gott mir nur gesundes Blut
So hab ich frohen Sinn!

Dies schrieb Dir Deine
Dich liebende
Freundin
Elfriede Haimoki

Dresden den 25.10.34

Dein Leben sei fröhlich und heiter
Kein Leiden betrübe Dein Herz,
Das Glück sei stets Dein Begleiter
Nie treffe Dich Kummer und Schmerz.

Dies schrieb Dir
Deine Freundin

Entries from my Autograph Book
—Jewish School, Dresden

And where is Elfriede Kaimsky, who wrote:

Why should I ask for riches and possessions
When I am content
If God will grant me health
I will be happy.

Where are all the children of that Jewish school on the second floor of the *Jüdische Gemeinde Haus* in Dresden?
Dead. Dead. Dead. Dead.

Opa and *Oma* Brach left Germany in 1936 and took up residence in a border town called Teplitz/Schönau in the Czech province of Bohemia. Ironically, we became the heirs of Bergstrasse Number 16 at a time when National Socialism had completely seeped into every fiber of the country, which was the reason for my grandparents' departure. Still, we moved into that lovely house like lords and ladies who would live there forever. My father even commissioned some interior architectural changes to accommodate us better. My eleventh birthday was celebrated there with a showing of black and white films. Uncle Emil, the man Berti had been introduced to and married through her new social connections with the Brachs, had a motion picture projector and a collection of film shorts suitable for children.

"Felix the Cat" was my favorite.

I remember the day in November 1937, when I saw Stitterich outside the school building standing at the side of the car.

What was he doing here, I wondered?

I had never been chauffeured home from school but always took the tram. When I asked him why he had come, he said, "Get in!" He slammed the doors, stepped on the accelerator and drove much faster than was his usual habit.

We are driving home, he said. I was to get my things and then he would drive me across the border. Nothing unusual about that part of it, I thought. It was Friday. But there was one thing that was exceedingly unusual. My parents had already left.

The feeling that something was odd, even ominous, was substantiated when we arrived at Bergstrasse Number 16. Gertrud, our maid at the time, was in a highly nervous state. She, too, was standing waiting for me. And now all she was doing was telling me to hurry. "Quickly, quickly!" "*Mach schnell, mach schnell!*"

I ran into my room. There, everything was packed. Why? I obviously didn't need all these things for a weekend trip. And then I knew.

"You think I'm never coming back?" I screamed. "Well, I will! You wait and see! I will! I'll be back before you know it!"

I opened my suitcases and threw everything on the floor.

"I'm not taking all this junk!" I yelled. "I don't need it. I'll take my toothbrush and that's all!"

Then I got into the car and drove off, with Gertrud standing at the door, tears in her eyes, trying not to show that she knew too.

Of course, I never came back. Never. And even if I did now, Bergstrasse Number 16 would be no more. It was destroyed by firebombs in 1945. So was Dresden. Stitterich and Gertrud have since died. And Hertha? Yes, I could still see her. But it would not be the same. Nothing was the same again from that moment on.

My grandparents' rented house in Teplitz/Schönau was no Bergstrasse Number 16. But it provided more than adequate shelter for us. Certainly, we were more fortunate than most who had skipped across the border without a penny in their pockets and no roof over their heads. And, of course, more fortunate than those who had been left behind. Uncle Isfried and uncle Rudi, my father's brothers for example, were taken to a concentration camp within the very week of our flight.

But if we had searched for a backdrop to reflect our shattered selves, we could hardly have found a more suitable one than Teplitz/Schönau. Sociologically and historically fractured, as many border towns are, with a German-speaking population that felt more identified with Germany proper than with Czechoslovakia, with soot-stained historic edifices turned into post offices and other bureaucratic facilities, Teplitz gave evidence that its past like ours, no longer existed. Even its mineral springs were depressing, and called "warrior baths," because soldiers with shotgun wounds were sent there by the former monarchs of France, Austria and Prussia.

But regardless of flight and impending immigration to America, an eleven-year-old girl has to go to school. I was enrolled in the II. *Mädchen Bürgerschule*, the public secondary school for girls, because it was within walking distance.

The II. *Mädchen Bürgerschule* turned out to be an institution which carried into the twentieth century the old and commonly held view that there are those who are born to rule and those who are born to follow. To make sure that this would always be the case, the society established an educational system which determined irrevocably the child's course in life, depending on the social standing of its parents. Entrance into secondary school was the great social way station. There, the wheat was clearly separated from the chaff and never the twain would meet. How could they? The boys whose parents had the social standing to send their sons to the *Gymnasium* were groomed for upper-class professions. Their female counterparts were sent to the *Pansionat* or finishing schools, to learn the social graces in preparation for becoming the wives of the boys who would automatically enter the universities.

But the boys and girls who went the other way, to the public secondary schools, were trained to become workers. The men primarily in factories, or at best as civil servants. The girls primarily as domestics, or possibly as nurses and seamstresses. If Bohemia had had a coastline, one more opportunity would have been open to the boys: to join the Navy as ordinary seamen, and stay in the fo'c'sle.

Opportunities for boys and girls to meet each other socially were built into the educational system of the upper classes. Social dances and balls were an accepted high point where the socially privileged got to know each other, danced and romanced with each other and later married each other. But in the public secondary schools, any fraternization between the sexes was rigorously excluded on the premise that the poorer classes were too sexually active.

When I walked up and down the corridors during recess with my black-stockinged and aproned girl classmates, curtseying whenever a teacher approached, and when I heard them giggling because a boy from upstairs, where the public secondary school for boys had its classes, had peeked through the stairwell door; and when I chanced to see such a boy, whose head was always shorn, on the presumption that the working classes lacked proper bathroom facilities and had lice—something about social harshness, privilege and lack thereof made its mark. Not that I really could sort it out intellectually at the time. Impressions were stronger than rational thought. As a matter of fact, I was failing all my subjects. Everything in that school seemed insurmountably difficult, particularly to me. I had had the privilege of asking questions in my former school experience. But in the II. *Mädchen Bürgerschule* we were force-fed, not unlike the Bohemian geese whose livers were sold at market. The approach was by rote—algebra, or embroidery, no matter. Exactness, preciseness, neatness were the requirements. No questions, ideas and feelings. No sense of discovery. After some months had passed, my report card clearly stated in stiletto script that I could not be promoted to the next grade.

In the confusion of this period, the oldest and the youngest members of my family had need for each other. My grandfather, no longer the head of state at Bergstrasse Number 16, marching in his park-like garden with his hands behind his back, would gently take me by the hand to wander thoughtfully through the streets of Teplitz. We usually headed in the direction of a distant mountain which had a castle atop. Although we never scaled the castle, nor even came close to it, it served as an important focus and enriched the many stories my grandfather would tell me while walking.

He had two kinds of stories. The first one was always set in the forest he knew as a boy in back of his hometown, Prerau, Moravia. This forest was called *die Kschiva*. K-s-c-h-i-v-a is the phonetic spelling of a Slavic word I know not the meaning of; *die* is the article which in German connotes the feminine. For whatever reason, etymological or otherwise, my grandfather's forest in his childhood town situated in the former Austro-Hungarian empire was symbolized as a woman.

My grandfather had always gone into the Kschiva in the afternoon when he was finished with school. "She" was always there. "She" never disappointed him. As soon as he entered, he knew something magical would happen, because "she" was an enchanted forest. As he walked in deeper and deeper, it would get darker, but he never lost his way, because he knew "she" would look out for him. Besides, he knew that "she" would not let him return until he had found something. What he was to find was her treasure, or a sample thereof. Something precious and glistening always lay buried within "her," and my grandfather would stumble upon what he described suspensefully as a precious stone, or a nugget of gold, seemingly by accident and just before he was expected home for dinner.

It was very important that he appeared in time for dinner, otherwise his parents would wonder where he was and sooner or later he would have had to tell them. But this way, he could keep "her" to himself. After all these years, it was a secret he had shared only with me while walking as exiles on the streets of Teplitz/Schönau.

The other kind of story was a quasi-lesson in geography and always led to natural wonders. Born in the 1870s, *Opa* Brach saw the world mainly in terms of its natural resources; its gold, its oil, its precious stones and minerals, and the great rivers and jungles which had to be forded in order to mine these treasures. His was a romantic nineteenth-century capitalism mixed with the dream of far off places.

He told me of Popocatepetl, the great snow-capped peak in Mexico and of Kilimanjaro, in Africa, where a railroad was being built. This was of particular interest to him because he had bought shares in this enterprise. But as far as we were concerned, the very best feature of a far off region was an unpredictable and active volcano. To us, this was the true indicator that the area was still palpitating with the primordial strength of mother nature, where a young nineteenth-century capitalist could make his fortune, mine "her" treasures and harness "her" for personal and collective profit in terms of industrial progress. It was *die Kschiva*, of my grandfather's boyhood. Though now that he was older, "she" was less of a benevolent mother figure who showed him wonders than an exciting young bride for him to "bridle."

Thus, while walking on the streets of Teplitz, our minds arched rainbow-like far beyond the darkening continent of Europe.

When the day's story was finished, the two of us would have to turn back: to my grandmother who was trying to run her household as if it were Bergstrasse Number 16; to my mother who was pregnant with my soon-to-be-born brother; to my father who was always listening to the radio for the latest political developments and worrying about daily delays in the red-tape immigration procedures at the American embassy in Prague; to my school whose instruction I could not follow.

In this period of extreme transition, yet another change had taken place. I had had my first menstrual flow. When it happened, I had locked myself into my grandmother's bathroom and would not come out for a long time. When my father briefly explained to me that I had not hurt myself, it did not make me happy. I was supposed to understand that the blood indicated my transition from child to young woman. But as far as I was concerned, the clocks were off. I felt more like a child than ever. One more major change was simply too much. I was not ready for it. If only the clock would stand still. No, not just stand still, but be set back.

That's when I first noticed the cracks on the pavement and stopped walking on them. With this came the inner voice, or compulsion to fold towels and napkins to perfection, edge on edge. To make everything super-even. And to touch tables and chairs while counting to eight at least. One, two, three, four, five, six, seven, eight. Eight taps on the back of a chair or the top of a table would help assure that "things would be all right." Ten taps would be better. Sometimes I felt I had to give twenty taps, just to make sure. Or, while sitting I would make myself get up ten times. Twenty table taps, ten times getting up and sitting down, five taps on the breakfront. And so it went.

The rituals had taken over. I was continually counting and tapping.

No one noticed.

Hitler was about to invade Austria. Time was running short. We left Teplitz and moved to Prague where my father tried to hasten our immigration at the American embassy. We lived temporarily in a newly built and not quite finished modern apartment complex. *Opa* Jakob and *Oma* Julia, my father's parents, were able to join us there. They received permission to leave Germany on account of their age, but their two sons, Isfried and Rudi, had to be left behind in a concentration camp. *Opa* Jakob, who had never been away from his hometown, continually prayed. *Oma* Julia took care of my baby brother (who had just been born), while my mother and I took English lessons. Our teacher was an American lady who had been living in Prague because she was in love with a Czech man who could not marry her. I am sure no one told me this, but the world then was full of adult whispers: who had skipped across the border, who had been left behind, who was able to get such and such a passport, how much did a citizenship cost?

One day the bell rang and three strange and crumpled-looking men asked for my father. Who were they? A father and his sons. Where had they come from? From Vienna just that moment. Hitler had invaded Austria the day before.

What did they want? Help.

I was standing behind the curtained glass door. I could feel their nervousness; their deathly anxiety. It was in their gestures, in their clothes, under their armpits and on their breath. I heard my father say Chinese passports were still for sale.

How much? How much?

Standing behind the glass door and staring at the three Jewish men, I wondered how they could ever become Chinese.

Henrietta Taylor, our American teacher, said that Americans were very practical. She demonstrated this by sticking toothpicks into a tomato and lettuce sandwich. She said this was an American invention to keep the filling from getting crushed and the sandwich from getting mushy.

She also noticed that I did not wash my socks, but wore the

same ones every day. "You have to wash your socks out at night," she instructed. "No one wears unwashed socks or underwear."

... A fact of life. Laundry had been of no concern to me. In Dresden I placed my clothes on a chair at night and the next morning Hertha or Gertrud, or whichever maid we had, had laid out a fresh set of underthings. My mother was as used to having her daily tasks performed for her as I. It fell upon a relative outsider to give me some pointers about how people lived in the New World—and in the real world.

I don't think I learned much English, but the toothpicks and the socks made a deep impression.

Before we boarded the boat in Genoa, we had a big family gathering in Switzerland. *Opa* Brach and *Oma* Luise were there. They were going to Cuba. Uncle Robert, my grandfather's brother and his wife, aunt Steffi, were there. They were going to Cuba too. *Opa* Jakob and *Oma* Julia were going to live with aunt Berti and uncle Emil in England. Uncle Fredi and his daughter, my cousin Ellen, were there, too. Ellen, a year younger than I, lived with her mother, Paula, in Bolzano, Italy.

It was thought that everyone there and, hopefully, also those who had been left behind, would eventually come to the United States. But my parents and I, with Tommy my baby brother, were to be the first to cross the water.

Summer 1938.

In Genoa we still had a few days left before boarding the *Conte de Savoia*. This gleaming Italian luxury liner, the sister ship of the famous *Rex*, was to take us to the New World. We spent the remaining days before departure living in the best hotel and spending money like water.

One of the things acquired was a beautiful gold bracelet which my father bought both as an investment and as a gift to my mother. He had seen it in a display case in the lobby of the Hotel Miramar and, putting his manicured forefinger against the glass, he had said, "I want this. How much?" My father had a habit of buying things right out of the window. My mother, on the other hand, had a habit of losing things. The bracelet was lost some time thereafter.

At the table next to us in the glass-enclosed dining room of the Miramar Hotel, sat a rich American. As the fresh figs in wooden crates (just like the *Calville* apples in Bergstrasse Number 16) were passed around, he engaged us in conversation and soon invited us to take a quick trip to Rome the next day in his private plane.

Why not? We had another two days to kill. Everything had been completed. A phase of our lives was finished. Just as in school, once we had handed in our term papers we were allowed to pass into the next phase. The future. For a brief time there was nothing more to do.

But dipping his hands in the finger bowl and gazing out on the shimmering Gulf of Genoa, my father declined. He was taking no chances. We had to get on that ship.

Even if circumstances had been different, he probably would not have accepted such a spontaneous invitation. Everything in my family was done by planning well ahead of time. Things were considered good *because* they had been well planned. Things were considered bad, *because* they had not been thoroughly thought through. Doing things on the spur of the moment, like flying to Rome for lunch, was not our style.

Leave things like that to those crazy Americans, my father

would say.

Those crazy Americans. Who were they? I would soon find out.

To set off for the new world my father packed white flannel trousers and linen Bermuda shorts. My mother, who was a passionate tennis player, wore white sports clothes. My brother, of course, was in white swaddling clothes. And I wore white shorts, a white polo shirt and a royal-blue school blazer with gold buttons. Dressed all in white, it seemed as though we were going on a cruise.

At the American consulate in Prague, I had seen Slavic peasants with babuschkas and bundles tied with string. They too had applied to go to America; they too had to fill out forms like us. But they were nowhere to be seen on our ship.

During the week-long ocean crossing, we played shuffleboard, swam in the pool and danced in the lounge at tea time. In the evening we watched American movies. Mr. Moto, a Confucius-quoting, English-speaking Chinese gentleman detective fascinated me most. As far as I knew, children in Germany only went to films which were approved for children to see, like "Felix the Cat" and movies with Shirley Temple, and never any films that had to do with crime. As a matter of fact, I believe these last were outlawed by the Nazi state as being foreign-made and decadent. Once I had seen an American western with Loretta Young and Gary Cooper. This was a harmlessly romantic film that adults went to see, and my mother was with me, of course. But I knew of the great stars of the Hollywood silver screen from looking at magazines, and collecting cards with pictures on them, which were given out by a manufacturer of mouthwash. Sylvia Sidney, Joan Crawford, Marlene Dietrich, Greta Garbo, Jean Harlowe were all familiar names and faces and were my most fascinating role models.

But Mr. Moto was different. His films were my first introduction to crime as entertainment—the British approach, where the elegantly dressed and learned gentleman outwits the more crude criminal through sheer intellectual superiority and coolness. Mr. Moto presented a clean, rational approach to the passion of crime, played and underplayed like a marvelous game of chess. The Age of Reason. Empiricism and Confucianism in the movies.

During the day, my mother frequently disappeared into the ship's kitchen where she would warm up my brother's bottle. I heard her tell my father that the kitchen staff called her *la bionda*, the blonde one. But my mother's hair was brown. I guess to the Mediterraneans, anyone with blue eyes was blond.

My father's idea of instant Americanization meant cursing in English. He would greet English-speaking persons on board with an emphatic, "God damn!" or "Go to hell!" From the painful smiles of the passengers, I sensed my father was making a fool of himself, but he seemed to enjoy it. The foreign language allowed him to say things he would never say in German, at least not to people like those he was addressing on board ship. Also, he knew he would be excused for supposedly not knowing better. But, of course, he did know better.

While this was going on—my father malpracticing his English and my mother drawing stares in the ship's kitchen—what was I doing? Just standing at the railing, looking out to sea and dreaming about a talent scout who would discover me on the streets of New York and take me to Hollywood.

The day before our arrival at the Port of New York, the 1938 hurricane struck. Already in the early morning, a heavy calm-before-the-storm sensation had settled on us, and a foreboding heaving and rolling was clearly at work below the surface of the sea. Right after breakfast, I curled into a deck chair and fell instantly asleep. When I woke up, my father was standing over me, his hair blowing every which way, shouting my name and shaking

Clockwise:
On board the *Conte de Savoia*
My father and I
My mother and I
My father and my brother Tommy

me out of my stupor. The boat was tilting, the dark gray leaden waves were crashing aboard. No one besides my father and I were left on deck.

I suppose, if he hadn't found me, I would have been tossed out to sea.

The next morning the sun was shining and our relatives, uncle Ferdinand and aunt Etta, were waiting for us at the pier. We were distantly related on my mother's side.

The reason they were there at all had to do with *Opa* Brach and one of his walks on the gravel paths of Bergstrasse Number 16. One day in the early thirties, while striding and talking to one of his entourage, *Opa* Brach decided that the time had come to open a branch of the malt empire in the United States. Prohibition had been lifted, and he saw no reason why he could not buy an old malt house somewhere in the New World.

If there had been another daughter to marry off, *Opa* Brach might have placed an ad in *The New York Times*, offering a wife and business partnership to some young American man. But since my mother had been the youngest and there were no more daughters, he dispatched uncle Ferdinand and aunt Etta to the United States to buy a malt house and start the business up. They were Hungarians and had lived in Budapest.

The National Malting Company, as the new business was called, was situated in Paterson, New Jersey, where uncle Ferdinand and aunt Etta had found a large former malt factory at a good price. No one thought that this branch would become our only means of support just a few years later when the *Hanna Maltzfabrik* in Olomouc , Czechoslavakia, and the *Elbschloss Maltzfabrik* in Schöna, near Dresden, were confiscated.

I had never met uncle Ferdinand before but aunt Etta had visited us in Dresden. She had talked a great deal about life in the United States, particularly about Klein's, a department store where she shopped for amazing bargains. I was fascinated by her information on how one could get something for almost nothing in New York, if one knew where to go.

Tales of how some American millionaires began by saving pennies they found on the street were also circulating in Dresden at the time.

Aunt Etta was nicknamed *Neger Tante*, or "Negro aunt," because she was very dark skinned. Real Negroes, as far as I knew, lived in Africa, though I had heard my father speak admiringly of someone named Josephine Baker, who he said was a beautiful dancer in Paris.

I had also seen pictures of Jesse Owens, who was a sensation at the Berlin Olympics in 1936. We had just gotten our first radio then and I had listened to reports of his feats.

And aunt Etta had spoken of someone by the name of Marian Anderson, who she said sang more beautifully than anyone she had ever heard in Europe.

But I had never heard of the Civil War, Abraham Lincoln, the South or anything like that. The United States to me that September day in 1938 meant: New York, Hollywood and President Franklin Delano Roosevelt.

For some reason, I do not recall getting off the ship, going through customs, or any details like that. I do not remember seeing the Statue of Liberty, or how it felt to first set foot in the New

World. None of these things registered. My mind didn't really start recording anything until we had settled ourselves into our relatives' car. It was aunt Etta who drove. There was no chauffeur. Maybe that was my first impression of the New World.

We must have made our way up the Westside Drive, but again nothing registered. I do not remember seeing the Hudson, tall buildings, or the George Washington Bridge, which certainly we crossed on our way to Paterson, New Jersey, where we were to live.

But what I do recall strongly was a subtle feeling, an attitude. Although we had been warmly welcomed, it seemed to me that we were being perceived by our distant relatives as we had never been perceived before: as persons who didn't know anything. I noticed that both aunt Etta and uncle Ferdinand talked to my parents as though they were children who had to learn things from scratch. This was strange indeed, particularly since members of my family were not inclined to doubt their positions and capacities. I had never witnessed anyone in my family admit to being unsure, or in need of advice, or being wrong, for that matter. They held strong opinions, based more on feeling than fact, and enjoyed asserting their wills.

Funny, that this subtle attitude was the only other thing that registered during our first ride in the New World. Not the Hudson River, not the marvel of the New York skyline, or the span of a great bridge; but the lack of a chauffeur and a peculiar feeling of being perceived differently here.

In Paterson, aunt Etta had readied an apartment for us in a two-storey wooden house on 775 14th Avenue, at the corner of Broadway. To us, the house had a peculiar architectural feature. All the other houses in Paterson seemed to have it too. It was called a porch. A rocking chair and a couch-like swing indicated that one could sit there and view life on the street. Heavens! Who would want to do that?

The verandas, gardens and yards in the houses I had known had all faced the back for greater privacy and seclusion. From my experience, one took great pains not to face the street side.

Bergstrasse Number 16, for example, had a tall, wrought-iron gate where private property met the street. If you wanted access to the house, you had to stand there and press a button. If you belonged to the family, or seemed to have a legitimate call, the maid, who could see you standing at the gate, would press the button on her end which opened the street gate. Next you walked past jasmine and rhododendron shrubs to the outside steps of the house. These led to a very tall portal which was then held open by a servant. This portal was the outside door of the house. It was immediately followed by a set of stairs which was carpeted and situated in a pink-marble-walled stairwell that led to the third door, the inside door of the house. Through it you entered into a large square atrium. Its floor was a mosaic of tiny black and white stones laid out in a Roman decorative pattern. Eighteenth-century engravings hung on ivory-colored walls.

From the glass-enclosed skylight two floors above, a soft muted light fell on four enormous leather club chairs surrounding a large table which formed the centerpiece of this Roman atrium.

Actually, the table was a bona fide casino roulette table which had somehow come with the house when it was purchased by *Opa* Brach. My grandmother kept it disguised with a large hand-embroidered cloth of dark wool.

The covered-up roulette table, which was never used by members of my family for what it had been originally intended, since none of them went in for gambling, was encircled by four dark brown leather club chairs, and served as the final checkpoint for legitimate callers who were not of the family. It was there they were asked to take a seat and to wait until someone else appeared to usher them into the inner sanctums of the house.

We had arrived. Now the only thing left to do was to get out of the car, walk up the thinly worn wooden steps, cross the porch and open the door. Then, without further preliminaries, we spilled into our new living room which had been sparsely furnished with aunt Etta's hand-me-downs.

Someone was sitting at the dining-room table. It was a quiet Negro girl. She was to be our maid.

Our landlord, Mr. Kaplan, and his two grown sons and one daughter, lived upstairs. They had come to America from Russia thirty years before us and they lost no time establishing that sensitive fact. It allowed them, as American citizens, to feel superior in every way to us, the newly arrived greenhorns. We had gotten a whiff of that particular attitude already from aunt Etta and uncle Ferdinand, but the Kaplans really rubbed it in. Mixed with their one-upmanship was an intense hatred for Germans, especially German Jews, who they said would have made the best Nazis if Hitler had let them.

Only my mother, who was born in Czechoslovakia and did not consider herself German, could ignore their slights. As a matter of fact she found something in common with these people, which my father and I never did. A great lover of music, my mother had had to leave her Steinway in Dresden, but Rose Kaplan had a piano upstairs and together they played four hands, while the two bachelor sons sang *Lieder*. German music was, apparently, all right with them. Not so were German names.

My mother allowed Rose Kaplan to enroll me in Public School No. 13. Having accepted that responsibility, Miss Kaplan gleefully rubbed out my name, registering me as Anne Hahn. She said that Hannelore was too Germanic. No one would know how to pronounce it, and I would never have any friends. I never felt comfortable as Anne, yet the name stuck with me through grammar and high school. I didn't get to be Hannelore again until college, when I felt I had the right to reclaim myself.

Once registered in P.S. No. 13, Anne Hahn was taken to Macy's to buy a school coat. That was the second trauma. How could it be that in the largest store in the world, not a single coat would fit? What was wrong with me, or the coats?

Finally, a camel-colored coat was found. It was marked "Chubby". The label seared me and stuck like a skewer in a pig. What had and would become of me? Was I Cinderella in reverse: the Dresden doll turned piggly-wiggly? How would I ever be discovered on the streets of New York and taken to Hollywood? How would anyone know that I was Hannelore, not Anne?

Contrary to the legend that in America everybody is somebody, I sensed that afternoon in Macy's Pre-Teen Department that in America, I, at least, was nobody.

But who were those somebodies? Those millions who could step into the ready-made clothes on the racks and walk out without a single alteration?

I was dying to find out.

The principal of Public School No. 13 was a Mrs. O'Byrne. I had never seen or heard a name like that before and couldn't imagine how to spell it. O'Byrne, O'Brian, O'Donnell, O'Dwyer, were completely foreign names to me. So were the Mc's and the

Mac's. Naturally, I soon learned that these were Irish, Scottish or English names; that a great many Americans were of Anglo-Saxon, or English extraction, and furthermore, that the Anglo-Saxons of the British Isles were not the Saxons I had known in Dresden.

My grandparents had a German police dog whom they called Lord. That name, plus *Oma* Luise's English tweed suits, were probably the closest I had ever come to anything English in Dresden.

Yes, these Anglo-Americans were the ones who could step into the ready-made clothes on the racks of the American stores and walk off without a single alteration! They were taller, longer-limbed and thinner than we. Their feet were so narrow they could wear a triple-A shoe, a size unheard of anywhere in Central Europe, I am sure. We, on the other hand, could not find shoes wide enough. Even a C-width would pinch. I was smitten with envy.

But aside from their physical characteristics, these Anglo-Americans behaved differently from us. They could be gracious without particularly loving or hating you. They knew how to be impersonal. We did not. We liked and disliked and let our feelings show. They did not. Like Mr. Moto, they seemed to act with consistent polite impartiality. Theirs was a code of behavior which seemed to have its origins in precepts of social intercourse which were totally alien to us. What was that code? Why did it seem so admirable? It did seem tremendously admirable to me.

In Europe, members of my family did not have to interact with anyone other than those with whom we were blood-related, and, of course, with servants. With both these categories, we felt secure. But here in America, there were so many categories and persons with whom one had to deal every day!

How does one deal with people who are neither family, nor servants? That was something we did not know.

Upon our arrival in Paterson, New Jersey, we found the city lying like an open sore, waiting for an industry to make its wheels spin as had been the early dream of Alexander Hamilton. I had not expected anything like that in America, the America I had seen in the Shirley Temple movies. Paterson was, as was the rest of the United States, in the grips of the Great Depression. What was this American phenomenon? We had only heard of America as a land of success. But America as a land of failure? Was that also part of the country we had come to live in?

The shock of this other view hit me full force whenever I visited my father in the National Malting Company on Governor and Ann Streets. It was frightening to go there, past empty lots and shutdown mills; past steely-eyed workers who mumbled obscenities; past liquor bottles in paper bags; past empty lots strewn with garbage; past wooden shanties on whose porches broken people rocked on broken chairs.

I remember the day my father came home from the office very distraught. He had had a visit from a representative of the labor union. Soon after our arrival, someone had lodged a complaint against him. I don't know what the specific grievance was, but it had something to do with his being too dictatorial.

My father had never had dealings with unions before. But he sensed their power and he feared them. What did they want from him? Didn't they know he had just come over from the other side?

That was just it. In this country we do things differently, Mr. Hahn, the union official said, substituting Mr. for Dr. Hahn, which was still what my father wished to be called. If you don't change, we'll call a strike.

Change? Was that in the minds of aunt Etta and uncle Ferdinand and the Kaplans upstairs? That we just were not right for this country? But what was wrong?

When Rose Kaplan registered me at P.S. 13, I was put into the 4th grade with children two years younger than me, because I did not know how to speak English. The class had a nine-year-old president and a nine-year-old secretary. They gravely presided over class meetings in which strict attention was paid to something I had never heard of before—Parliamentary Procedure. Often discussion on an issue bogged down because something was out of line with the parliamentary rules. I could not understand why we could not just go on and forget about motions, quorums and other fine points of procedure. This was not a question of not knowing enough English. It was a question of not understanding heritage and tradition, history and ideology, which were also English.

Mr. Moto, the gentleman detective, for example, did not avoid the subject of crime on the basis that it was too sordid for a gentleman like him. No, he remained the gentleman by applying to a sordid subject a gentlemanly code. He demonstrated that the approach and the procedure are just as important as and sometimes more so than. the subject itself.

Why should the "how" take precedence over the "what"? I could not fathom it. How things were done, I thought, was only important in terms of manners. One did not eat with elbows on the table, one stood up for elderly persons, one did not spit on the floor. Good manners showed breeding and breeding exemplified class. It was as natural as breathing to me that one was born into a class; a social class.

But in the 4th grade class at Public School No. 13 in Paterson, New Jersey, I sensed something else. Something about that parliamentary procedure and the emphasis that was placed on it communicated to me that something vital was at stake. Even if the end was good and worthy, if one had gotten there by using unacceptable means, the Anglo-Saxons would rather not get there at all or so it seemed to me: MEANS vs. END.

Another new-to-me concept cropped up again and again. Ideas were considered worthless in America unless one could implement them: PRAGMATISM.

In America, I heard people say, "Yes, it's a good idea, but how are you going to make it work?" What difference does that make, I wondered. It wasn't our job to make things work. Workers did that. Isn't it enough to have an idea? Ideas were inspirational: INDUCTIVE vs. DEDUCTIVE THINKING.

Superior persons had ideas: ELITISM vs. DEMOCRACY.

Anyone could implement them: ENGINEERING vs. ABSTRACT THINKING.

We would say, "It's a good idea." Why? Because we believed in it. If we didn't believe in it, it wasn't a good idea. None of us would spend time or energy on something we didn't believe in first. But in America people said, "Anyone can have an idea. Ideas are a dime a dozen. Making them work is what counts.": BRASS TACKS vs. THEORY.

Opinions my family had plenty of. It seemed we were born with them and felt we had a right to hold them. But in America, opinions were constantly challenged and had to be substantiated by fact: OBJECTIVE vs. SUBJECTIVE.

I had never heard of these words before either, and they gave me a lot of trouble. "Don't be so subjective," I would be told. "Don't jump to conclusions. Be specific. Get down to brass tacks. Don't take things so seriously."

People in America were always bringing things down to specifics. We, on the other had, preferred to rise to lofty conclusions. Quantitative thinking—how much, how many—did not come natural to us.

There was something else I did not do. I did not think in terms of plurals. I never thought of "people." I was conditioned to the one-to-one relationship—individuals, not groups.

Buying that first coat at Macy's exemplified our total experience of coming to the United States: The individual vs. the collective. One body vs. one-million coats. Not one of them would fit. Trying to find something that fits and not finding it; then, in turn, trying to fit ourselves into the modes and sizes of the new land.

A tall order.

Having always had everything custom-made, we did not know our physical sizes, and when we learned them, we found that America did not have us in mind when it made overcoats, dresses and shoes. In the realm of ideas and values, the matter was the same, though in reverse. For we discovered that we did not have America in our minds and in our ways of thinking. To put it plainly: we, who ourselves had fled from oppression, had no knowledge of Democracy.

Squeezing.

That's what I did every day when I came home from school for lunch. I would squeeze into one of the benches in our tiny kitchenette. It always was a tight squeeze because the table was too wide. My mother would set a low-calorie salad in front of me, which was an attempt to slim me down to the American dimensions. To supplement my "diet," I would listen to "The Affairs of Helen Trent" on the radio.

School was my main arena for learning how to squeeze into the American mold. It seemed as if P.S. No. 13 had been waiting for a student like me. I arrived there, I suppose, with uncommon eagerness; that special energy which immigrants surely had before me, when upon crossing the water and finally setting foot on the new land, they wanted above all else to become a part of it, to embrace it and to be embraced by it. This was truly the time for the fresh start. The slate had been wiped clean.

No wonder I liked watching the teacher wipe the slate. It was one of my favorite moments. I compared the American method of slate wiping with the European one. The American method was the dry one: it employed a felt wiper. The European method was wet: it depended on a sponge and water. The American method was faster, but the Eurpoean one left a cleaner slate. On the other hand, the American classrooms had many more slates. This enabled the American teacher to walk from slate to slate, without ever having to wipe the board until the janitor did it at the end of the day. A concept from industry applied to other areas: DIVISION OF LABOR.

I had learned to speak English effortlessly within four months, and within two years I had skipped four times, winning every honor P.S. No. 13 could bestow, including a certificate from the Palmer Method for penmanship. The Palmer Method was taught in the Paterson school district with the anticipated result that everyone's handwriting would look alike. The method emphasized light gliding strokes slanted toward the right and was about as different from my straight, pointy and heavy-pressured German script as figure skating is from jousting with heavy armor. Anne Hahn at age eleven, twelve and thirteen willingly gave up her script, even her name, in her devoted effort to become "American."

Once a year, the school children had a day in Paterson's City Hall. Those children deemed to be the best candidates for civic posts were elected by both their classmates and their teachers. I was elected to be Attorney General and joined by fellow officials—the child Mayor, the child Director of the Budget, the child Sheriff (without myself knowing what an Attorney General was)—at City Hall. There I sat in court listening to an obese lady state her complaint against a beauty parlor whose faulty drier had, allegedly, burned her hair.

The word "allegedly" stood out. Although the accusor's hair was clearly singed, the accused was deemed innocent unless proven guilty. How different from the law my father knew. His law was based on Roman law which presumed that the accused was guilty unless proven innocent. How much more on the side of the common person that Anglo Saxon law was, the law of my new land: the country of, by and for the people. And, indirectly, this gave me hope. In America, I felt I would do great things one day.

I joined the Girl Scouts and became a Tenderfoot in Troop No. 10 spending summers at Camp Te Ata near Suffern, N.Y. There I learned how to fold the American flag after taking it down from the flagpole at night, how to give first aid, how to tie a tourniquet, make a splint, save a life from snake bite and how to give artificial respiration.

I learned how to make a campfire with sticks and one match and how to roast marshmallows, cook eggs-on-a-rock and pigs-in-blankets.

I learned songs like "Greensleeves" and other Anglo Saxon and American rounds: "The Golden Day Is Dying," "Come, Follow, Follow," "Whip-Poor-Will," "The Keeper," "Green Grow the Rushes," as well as Negro spirituals like "Every Time I Feel the Spirit."

I also gained fifteen pounds. The menu at Camp Te Ata consisted mainly of baked macaroni with cheese, baked beans with corn bread, and a dessert called "Mississippi Mud," a starchy chocolate pudding which the Black cook dished out from oblong enamel pans and slapped into individual serving bowls with a large spoon.

I was always hungry.

In America my father was always tired. He would come home exhausted from the office, have dinner and then switch on the radio to listen to "Major Bowes," or "Gangbusters," his favorite programs.

My father was an ambitious man. All the more strange that in a land where men's most ambitious dreams became reality, he could not see his future.

While I was trying to squeeze into the mold of the new country, pledging allegiance to the flag, selling Girl Scout cookies and learning how to tie square knots, my father slowly squeezed out. His ambitions had been realized in Europe. He had climbed the ladder of success; from small town to corporate executive.

But that didn't mean anything here. America wipes the slate clean.

This erasing of the past, which was no doubt a blessing to millions who carried no past glories with them, was no blessing to my father. He felt he had achieved status in Europe and he held on to the crown jewel of his past: PRIVILEGE.

My father's need to emphasize his station was illustrated, for example, by his continued insistence on being called "Dr. Hahn." True, he had earned the title in law school at the University of Würzburg, with a doctoral dissertation on the legal rights of prisoners-of-war, but in America lawyers were not called doctors. To make matters worse, my father had never practiced law professionally. Therefore, holding on to such a title in the new country was even more unjustified.

In a country of pragmatism, one does not hold title without performance of its duties.

In a democracy, there is no rank without responsibility.

No wonder my father surrounded himself with his old cohorts from "the other side," who were now living in Washington Heights, in northern Manhattan. They used to visit us in droves on Sundays, taking the bus across the George Washington Bridge and enjoying a day in what they called the "country."

In business, my father also relied on his European and foreign contacts. Thanks to his salesmanship, the National Malting Company flourished, though its customers were not the domestic

Paterson New Jersey:

Clockwise from lower left:
Lawrence and River Street, Paterson,
 New Jersey. Photo credit: George A. Tice
The newly arrived immigrants on the steps of
 their new home, Paterson, New Jersey
Our first American car

National Malting Company
NaMaCo

brewers. They were the German and Latin-American brewers in Brazil, Argentina, Nicaragua and Honduras, to whom 90% of our malt was sold.

One day, my father actually arrived from south of the border with a new title. It was "Consul Dr. Arthur Hahn." The title was strictly honorary and carried no portfolio, but it allowed him to bypass the American melting pot.

Actually, what really perplexed us in the New World was a paradox. On the one hand, the New World's physical immensity offered a sense of freedom of movement which beckoned to be traversed without restrictions. We could understand and enjoy the physical mobility of being able to travel long distances without needing passports and visas, because all that enormous territory belonged to "us."

But social mobility was something else. True, a "nobody" could become a "somebody" in a relatively short period of time, by knowing something very well, working hard and being in the right place at the right time. But this did not mean that the social landscape of the country was entirely without restrictions. We, who did not know the deeper structure of America, misjudged its freedoms as license. What we were not prepared for, in other words, was the fact that alongside mobility was a strong framework of accepted behavior based on Anglo-Saxon democratic principles. Freedom of speech, yes. But if one voiced prejudice of class, or was dictatorial, one had better be prepared for criticism. We were not prepared to be judged.

Nor were we prepared for yet another side of the new land we had come to, its public side. While on the one hand, America was the country that stood for individual rights and freedoms, we found, on the other, that it also exerted strong public pressure upon the individual. And this pressure was primarily a pressure to conform. Henry Ford was to have said about the Model-T that anyone could buy it in any color as long as it was black.

If in the area of manufacture standardization was necessary, it was overdone, we thought, in other areas that had nothing to do with the manufacture and production of goods. American thinking, we found looked for the average, the rule, the norm and the many, whereas our thinking first picked out the exception. Thus, to us, the United States in the late thirties and early forties was "Palmer Method" all the way.

I had one friend my age. Her name was Kim Webber. Kim lived in an apartment house which had a lobby that was decorated to look like a Tudor English castle. Apartment house lobbies in the New World always astounded me. They tried to make an extraordinary impression and misled you into expecting similar grandeur upstairs, which was often not the case.

Kim always wore a key on a chain around her neck which she would use to open the door of her tiny apartment when she got home from school. Her mother was divorced and did not come home from her job until later. She would leave notes for her daughter on the kitchen table. *Buy a carton of milk, get a loaf of bread* the notes would say.

Kim and I became friends, I suppose, because we were both lonely. Loneliness had become my daily companion in the New World.

Kim wrote in my diary;

"Dear Hannelore,
Remember the girl from the city
Remember the girl from the town
Remember the girl who spoiled your book
            ·uʍop ǝpᴉsdn ᵷuᴉʇᴉɹʍ ʎq
Your friend Kim Webber, U.S.A.
June 23, 1940, Paterson, New Jersey"

Where was Isolde Elber?
Where was Elfriede Kaimsky?
Where was Wera Bernstein?

None of us said it. None of us would even have dared think it. But since coming to the United States, no one in my family was really happy. We were intense patriots and any expression of dissatisfaction with our life in the New World would have been considered sinful. Wasn't this the best country in the world? Wasn't this the country the millions of people we left behind would die to come to? Wouldn't just about anyone in Europe change places with us immediately, if they could? And what would have happened to us if we had stayed? It was unthinkable.

But something was wrong.

Then came the incident with the fuses. A fuse had blown out in our apartment and my father went into the cellar to see what he could do. I was to stay upstairs and let him know by shouting down the cellar steps when the lights went on, or off, or whatever effect his tampering with the fuse box was having.

This was probably the first time my father had ever had to fix a fuse. He had been conditioned to have all handywork done by the so-called workers. His avoidance of doing things for himself had even gone so far in Dresden as to his having a barber come into the house every morning to shave him.

Somehow, my father and I got our signals crossed. Whatever

he had called up from the cellar, I misunderstood. When the lights had gone back on I called "yes!" but in the meantime he had done something else and the lights had gone out, and so it went back and forth. Our signals would not synchronize. Finally, my father came up from the cellar heaving with a blind rage, and struck me again and again.

The trouble between me and my father had started.

The one do-it-yourself concession my father did make in the New World was to learn how to drive. Our first car was a black Plymouth sedan. Every Sunday we took a long drive, usually to Bear Mountain.

My mother and father would sit in front and my little brother, Tommy, and I would sit in the back. Occasionally, my father would glance into his rear-view mirror and ask why I was so quiet. I would answer that I was thinking.

"Well, can't you share your thoughts with me?" he would ask.

"No, I can't" would be my reply.

Communication between us had been cut. A fuse had blown.

What I was actually doing was dreaming. Particularly on the way back from our Sunday outings, when it was getting dark and warm lights glowed in the houses we passed, I was wishing for my place in a beautiful future. Those neat little homes we passed appeared to me to have in them nice American families who were all settled and secure. Like the Forbeses, for example, a Catholic family in Paterson, who had five children and whose girls were forever washing and ironing their cotton dresses. I don't know what there was about those cotton dresses. But there was something about that perpetual laundering, bleaching, starching and pressing, that perpetual hanging on hangers and being ready for the next day, which convinced me that the Forbeses believed in something the next day would bring and that they were getting ready for.

The future. Yes, that's what I was dreaming of while we were driving past cozy American homes in our first American car, in a silence which was heavy and foreboding and broken only by the news on the car radio.

Europe was involved in the Second World War.